SALES &
MARKETING
IN THE
DIGITAL AGE

Howard Tullman

Published in the United States of America
For bulk orders, please contact info@blogintobook.com

Perspiration Principles logo designed by James "Red" Schmitt
Special Thanks to Lakshmi Shenoy and Claudia Saric

To purchase all volumes of The Perspiration Principles, please visit:
BlogIntoBook.com/tullman/

ISBN13 - 9781619849822
ISBN10 - 1619849828

DEDICATION

Sitting down every week to write something that will be meaningful and ideally of lasting value to others is a lot like setting out to start a new business. Sometimes there's a germ of an idea; sometimes it's an emotional reaction or other driver; or perhaps it's just a problem or situation that needs to be addressed. And occasionally you simply want to see things change and no one else is stepping up to the plate to make that happen.

You can't know how hard, long or costly (in many ways) the journey will be and there are no guarantees that anything good will ever come of your efforts, but you know for certain that nothing will ever happen if you don't get the process started and try. It's a lonely path and every bit of encouragement, assistance and support that you find along the way makes the job a little easier and slightly more likely to succeed.

I hope that these books will be my modest contribution to your success and to the well-worn and tattered bag of hopes and dreams which we call entrepreneurship.

CONTENTS

YOU CAN'T SAVE YOUR WAY TO SUCCESS

Every business owner understands that, in addition to the many internal factors which can make or break a business, the cyclical state of the economy itself can also have a material impact on the success of your company. To a certain extent, it's like the weather - we can bitch about it all we want and blame those no-good politicians, but - in the end - we have only a limited ability to change these external market conditions. However, that doesn't mean that anyone should be sitting around feeling sorry for themselves and waiting for their life to get better.

I love the old Chinese saying: "Man stand for long time with mouth open before roast duck fly in". Good things in business don't happen by themselves (except perhaps in the movies) and, if you aren't making things happen and moving forward, you'll always be losing ground. So, in my world, we don't whine about politics, circumstances or greener grass. We believe that the people who succeed in today's hyper-competitive marketplace are the ones who get up and look for the right "circumstances" and, if they can't find them, they make them. Everyone thinks about changing the world, but no one thinks about changing themselves or their business. But, as I've said before, if you don't do it, someone will come right along who'll be very happy to do it for you or to you.

We've been treading water for too long and FUD (fear, uncertainty and doubt) has made us way too conservative. The big guys have been cutting back on their R & D budgets for years to protect pennies of earnings and thereby killing any prospects for new ideas and real innovation. And the little guys (like us) have been saving our shekels and not advertising or promoting our businesses. We need to start investing aggressively in the future (like we really mean it) or many of us won't have a future to worry about.

Now's the time to push our products and services and to demonstrate to everyone that we have the courage of our convictions. Not when the whole world finally wakes up and jumps back into the fray. I like to think of this running ahead of the pack as "getting ready to get lucky".

And, when you press your bets and bet on yourself and your future, you actually accomplish three other important objectives:

(1) You effectively set the pace for the rest of the market and you can become the market leader even if you're a tiny company;

(2) You reassure not only your customers, but your employees and your vendors as well; and

(3) You can grow your business at the expense of your competition without spending a lot of money since they've pretty much left the playing field to you.

Keep in mind this simple fact: increased market share is taken and grown NOT in good times, but in difficult times when everyone else is sitting on the sidelines and nursing their wounds. In good times, people want to advertise. In bad times, they have to advertise.

If you don't, you die. The minute you hit the brakes, you start to slide down the sales slope.

Here's a case in point concerning Saturn.

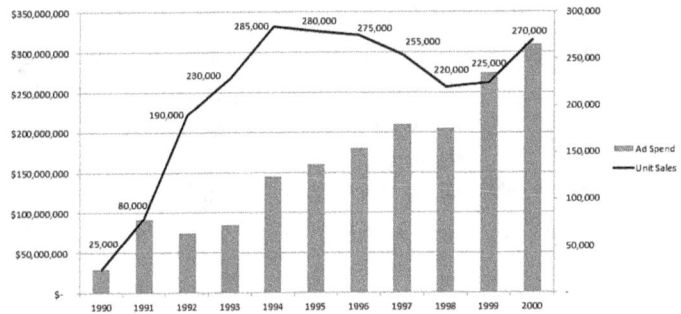

When sales dipped a tiny amount at the start of 1995, they started to cut their ad spending and that flattened 1995 and 1996 sales. Then they tried to get back into the game heading into 1997, but panicked when the sales didn't immediately recover and they cut back again on the ad spend. This killed not only 1997 results, but 1998 and 1999 sales as well even though they really accelerated their spend in mid-98. The bottom line (as the chart clearly shows) is that trying to "save your way to success" (or even to improved bottom line results) is like trying to catch a knife. Most of the time, you just can't do it and it's very painful even when you do.

And here's a little survey of 600 U.S. companies whose revenues increased after the 1981-82 recession and what they did with their advertising during the recession.

Companies <u>Increasing</u> Advertising – VOLUME UP 275%

Companies <u>Decreasing</u> Advertising – VOLUME UP 19%

It couldn't be much clearer. Ya gotta spend real money to make money. Doing business without advertising is like winking at a girl in the dark – you know what you're doing, but no one else does. And please don't try to do a bunch of things cheaply that you shouldn't do at all.

Bottom line: get going. There are a number of things – large and small - that every business should do right now (especially if you believe that there's even a glimmer of light at the end of this long dark tunnel) to prepare for the better days to come. But there's one thing that is absolutely critical to understand - in good times to be sure, but even more so in tough times - you can't save your way to success.

DATA IS THE OIL OF
THE DIGITAL AGE

I said two years ago that - by 2020 - 90% of the U.S. population would have willingly agreed to provide at least some of their personal data to the MAW. I'm starting to think that my estimate was too conservative. The global pace of massive data acquisition is picking up steam and speed and it's definitely an auto-catalytic process - the faster the changes come at us, the sooner the next changes start to appear. So you need to get moving just to hang on.

There are many explanations for the acceleration, but the main and most important change seems to be that no one expected that all of the diverse behavior drivers (inducements, incentives, trade-offs, etc.) would converge on each of us so quickly, specifically, simultaneously and, frankly, pretty much inescapably. But that's where we're at - stuck in the middle of the M.A.W.- and getting in deeper every day.

The M.A.W. - in case you're wondering - is my shorthand for today's replacement for that tired old whipping boy - the evil military-industrial complex - which we were all told - dictated and controlled our lives. The M.A.W. is slightly more benign so far in that it doesn't so much control our lives every day as it engulfs and overwhelms us 24/7 with emotional and economic sticks and carrots which continually impact and influence our behavior.

The M.A.W. (the omnipresent collision of (M)edia, (A) dvertising, and (W)ork in every part of our lives) is the real environment in which we're all now living. And honestly we've all become willing participants (to varying degrees) in the program and relatively happy campers with the deals we're making and the results because no one wants to be left out or left behind. Springsteen said "we're livin' in the future and none of this has happened yet", but he was wrong. It's happening right now.

And, by the way, this is another party to which I hope you're not waiting for an invitation. You and your team need to get into the data marketplace with both feet before your business get priced out of the game by greedy middlemen happy to resell the data to you at a premium (DSPs and others) and before you get shut out of the market entirely by faster and deeper-pocketed competitors who will absorb all the available inventory.

Keep in mind that the key notion above is that "we agreed" to share and surrender this information. God only knows how much of our own information we have inadvertently or unwittingly parted with at this point in time. I'm simply talking about the extent to which each of us has made a deal - a conscious transaction - where we have decided to trade and supply some of our personal data in exchange for some perceived value or benefit that we would be receiving in return. And by the way I don't mean "perceived value" in the pejorative sense as if these things weren't real and concrete. For sure, some incentives are virtual and slight at best (like digital badges and certain utterly inconsequential "achievements"), but many others have clear and direct financial and economic benefits.

What kinds of value or benefits are we talking about? The list grows daily. You trade your personal data because:

a. We're all basically lazy and would rather do less work than more – Do It for Me is a lot easier than DIY;

b. We hate wasting our time and re-entering the same info over and over in order to perform recurring activities of any kind;

c. We become "invested" in an activity as a result of our prior effort and commitment and we just tend (due to inertia) to keep going with the flow;

d. We've "connected" with others who are important to us in a shared context through the activity and it becomes convenient to continue and difficult to depart;

e. We develop habitual behaviors and habits (online or otherwise) are just really difficult to break or abandon without a reason;

f. We're actively "engaged" and "retained" by the smartest of the players so we stay; and/or

g. We receive direct financial rewards for our participation.

When you add these up, we're talking about saving you time, making you more efficient or productive, connecting you with a community or group that's valuable to you; or that old stand-by – making you or saving you money. In many of the cases, it does basically come down to money. Almost everything does.

One of the neatest new deals has been created by a couple of the largest auto insurers in the U.S. If you let Allstate (thru its *Drivewise* program) or Progressive (thru the *Snapshot* offering) track your driving activities for a relatively short period of time, you can earn major discounts on your car insurance. It's a "win-win" for anyone who's a decent driver. I call this "swapping surveillance for savings". And we can expect to see more and more offers and opportunities like this.

It's pretty easy with tools like *FitBit* and other biomedical tracking devices to think that many of our daily activities will soon be available for researchers, marketers, economists, behaviorists, etc. to pay us for and acquire in order to study and sell.

And, by the way, it's definitely a two-way street. You can also pay up to be left alone. If you're sick of being swamped with ads on your Kindle, you can pay up and cut them off. At the end of the day, it's all just math and money.

But here's the bottom line. We're all involved in competitive markets today and it's really an arms race which will be won by the guys with the biggest guns, the best technology, and, above all, the most accurate and complete data.

Think of this as fair warning – your competitors are grabbing the goods and dropping big dollars for data and, if you don't want to be left in the dust, you need to get into the game as well.

FORGET MADE-UP METRICS & FALSE FACTS

Microsoft Excel is a curse. In its deceptive simplicity and ease of use, it has taught several generations of MBAs and entrepreneurs that creating the financial underpinnings for a serious business plan is basically just another form of word processing. It has insulated these aspiring business builders from the difficult and time-consuming - step-by-step - tasks of building a real case for a real business from the bottom up. Making a plan for the future without tying your analysis to the concrete experiences, results, and wisdom of the past is just a form of building castles in the sky.

As a result of the Excel explosion, we've seen the creation of thousands of mindless spreadsheets underlying hundreds of naïve business plans put forward by individuals who have relied on Excel to painlessly develop forecasts and predictions which haven't the slightest connection to any reality, but which look "marvelous" as Billy Crystal used to say. And then these folks (and their promoters, investors and enablers as well) seize upon these plans as if they were the Gospel expressed in rows, columns, and pivot tables and use them for support and borrowed credibility - rather than for analysis, guidance and hoped-for illumination – exactly the same way that a late night drunk relies on a lamppost. Welcome to the fantasy world of made-up metrics.

When you use a tool like Excel (that's fundamentally neutral) to generate hypothetical and hysterical numbers to make a theoretical case with no real foundation in fact or history and then you fall in love with the finished product, you're deeply into made-up metrics. Credible plans need to proceed from a serious grounding in prior, documented experience and results – they can extend those results into the future – I would call these "projections" and, while they are never certain, at least they are logical and well thought out. We used to call this process "precision guesswork", but at least we had a process and we knew where our numbers came from. "Predictions", on the other hand, are the results of those cases where people simply insert aggressive new growth numbers (without any clear justification, obvious cause, or decent explanation) and then use Excel to replicate, grow and run the numbers forward until they reach the sky.

When you get carried away with this approach, you tend to forget that building a real business is about producing results, not predicting results. It's actually easy to predict the future, it's just impossible to know when it will arrive. You can plan all the plans you wish, but you can't plan results – you have to do the hard work of making those happen – and that hard work starts with building a solid factual foundation for your numbers. Too many excellent Excel plans are just sterile exercises stuck somewhere between wishful thinking and delusion.

Another entire category of bogus business plans are crammed with so many fake facts and factoids and other accumulations of data that are only remotely relevant at best to the business being built. Grossed-up market size is always one of my favorites. "Our addressable market is everyone with two eyes in the world." Right. Fake facts are all the rage these days, but they don't help advance your cause. I think Seth Godin is a smart and thoughtful guy, but here's what he had to say in a recent blog post: "[Aside: More than a billion people on Earth have never purchased anything on sale at a store.]" Do you really think there's any factual basis for that statement? Why waste our time with this kind of stuff?

Even good facts are just facts – they're not props for arguments or support for conclusions – it's the conditions, trends, needs, and other market circumstances that you extract and extrapolate from the facts that help to explain, define and ultimately "sell" your business idea to investors, customers and partners. It's these larger drivers which you need to discover, document and master – and not cute anecdotes and fake facts – that will provide the real framework for the continual decisions you'll need to make as you move things forward.

Building a business in these tough times is about pushing your vision forward and adapting it where necessary through a sea of constantly changing facts and circumstances. But if you don't start with a fundamental idea – grounded in some reality – it's way too easy to get run around in circles or just lost in the shuffle. These are serious problems for young entrepreneurs because the triumph of the form of the materials over their real substance (slick spreadsheets) and misplaced reliance on irrelevant metrics (fake facts) can lead you to believe that you have your arms around your business when – in fact – you're swinging a big hammer, but you're trying to nail *Jello* to a tree.

WHEN THE ELEPHANTS DANCE, IT'S THE GRASS THAT TAKES A BEATING

It's downright dangerous for small companies (and especially start-ups) to deal with the corporate giants who dominate so many industries. They're the pachyderms; we're the plant life. And like elephants, they have great memories and recall how the world was; but no imaginations to see the world that will be. Still, because of the size of their markets; the fact that so many of them are dinosaurs who don't see the deluge about to drown them; and the fact that timely innovations and new technologies will ultimately turn their businesses around or put them in the ground, these are the places where the people who want to be real players need to be.

Entrepreneurs with great ideas and enormous energy (but limited time, resources and access) face a number of specific challenges in circumstances like these, but there are 5 things to keep in mind which can dramatically improve your odds of success.

1. Right Church - Wrong Pew

It's easy to get lost or misdirected when you're wandering through the wastelands of these large companies. Too often people with new ideas get sent to (not to say "dumped on") the new media, innovation or digital guys and quickly forgotten. Typically the people who populate these departments are long on enthusiasm and short on cash and the ability to green light anything. It's critical to remember that big firms have many different pockets of serious money. If you spin your story correctly, you can often tap into community programs, marketing initiatives, charitable commitments or even diversity requirements – all of which are well-funded. Don't be shy about asking – sometimes success is simply putting a new cover on the same old book - or adding a novel twist to an old tale. But make sure before you start that you're in the right place.

2. Right Pew - Wrong Seat

Even if you're in the right place with the right story, your proposal still needs to "fit" the customer's current interest and appetite. You need to make sure that what you're offering matters. This means that – when all is said and done – and you've busted your butt and hit it out of the park – and you've done it all with panache and a vengeance – you don't want to hear those two awful words from the client: "So what?" or something equally disappointing. You need to make sure that you understand the required size, scale and impact which will be needed to <u>matter</u> – to impress the client and his bosses – and to move the needle for them or you'll just have been wasting a lot of your time and energy. The problem is that even great results (high adoption percentages, significant engagement times, strong sharing and amplification, etc.) which are hugely significant and encouraging to the entrepreneur just don't matter if you're talking hundreds of active participants in your pilot and they're dealing with millions of card members or customers. I've seen major retailers do this over and over – they'll run almost any credible pilot project (especially one on your dime) for a new service or product, but they won't pull the trigger when the project is done because their metrics don't match yours.

And, if that wasn't bad enough, keep in mind that while start-ups run out of cash – big companies don't – and so they are more than happy to keep mediocre projects running for way too long – even though they may have mentally checked out some time ago.

3.   Right Seat - Wrong Guy

Another recurring risk in dealing with big businesses is that the guy sitting across from you can't say "yes". There are hundreds of people in these places who can say "no" – some of whom seem to have no other job than that – but you've got to get in front of the ones who can say "yes" and write the necessary check to put their money where their mouth is. As I have said before, you don't want to be dealing with the monkey when the organ grinder is in the room.

You've also got to be sure that you carefully explain how your proposal is incremental and additive to whatever it is that they are now doing and that it's not simply going to cannibalize their current sales or replace existing sales with less lucrative or valuable ones. We used to call these "kissing your sister" deals because they don't lead anywhere you'd want to be and you have a lot of motion and activity but no real progress or results.

4.   Right Guy - Wrong Time

I'm always amazed at how many entrepreneurs don't do their homework and understand the budget and buying cycles of their target customers and how these things are set in concrete and so tightly locked down that these people couldn't help you if their lives depended on it. I think this is because there really are no comparable restraints or barriers in the life of a start-up – everything is urgent, everything can be and needs to be done right now, and there's always no time like the present to do what needs to be done. But bad timing can be the quickest deal killer of all and – more to the point – if you show up at the wrong time, it's pretty obvious to the customer that you don't know much about their business, their calendars or their requirements. Don't make this amateur mistake.

There is one exception to this rule and that depends almost entirely on whether or not you have been lucky enough to develop a real connection and relationship with your buyer. If you have, then on occasion you will tumble into the *Alice in Wonderland* scenario where the buyer lets you know that – instead of their budgeted funds being totally committed and/or spent - they have excess funds which they need to spend before their budget year runs out to avoid having their budget cut for the following year. All I can say about these situations is – take the money and run.

5. <u>Right Time – Wrong Pitch</u>

Sometimes the best way to get the order is not to try selling at all, but simply to focus on "helping" the customer understand the competitive dynamics of their marketplace. Fear is rampant in even the biggest companies and the greatest fear for many decision-makers is FOMO. The Fear Of Missing Out. Many market resources and opportunities are scarce or finite and letting these big guys know that there are other major players in the space who are about to shut them out is a very substantial and effective motivator.

One of my favorite old examples involves what I call cross-industry blocking alliances. These are cases where major players in different vertical market team up in a competitive game of musical chairs and the last company to find a chair (actually a partner) loses out big time and potentially for years thereafter. One of the great marketers of all times – American Express – was an early victim of this strategy and it cost the company millions of cardholders and billions of dollars. The story is very simple.

In the early days of frequent flyer programs, a very smart guy at American Airlines determined that miles could be used as an incentive not simply for flying, but for many other things (like car rentals and credit card purchases) as well. American quickly and quietly partnered with MasterCard. United in a flash (almost) partnered with VISA. And guess where that left American Express. Out in the cold without an airline partner which was credible and widely-available for business travelers. I suppose they could have partnered with Midway Airlines or with Greyhound and covered the bus market, but basically they were screwed for years. In the next several years, while AMEX topped out at about 9 million cardholders, VISA blew right by them and grew to almost 30 million cardholders in the same timeframe.

MAKE SOMETHING THAT MATTERS

I like to be supportive of almost any implementations of new, exciting technologies – even when I think that some are definitely "solutions in search of a problem" or the latest and greatest examples of "software that only the designer's mother could love", but there are limits and sometimes you see something so sad; so ill-conceived; and so poorly executed that you have to speak out just to avoid all of us toiling in these fields from being tarred and feathered with the same brush or beaten over the head with the stupid stick.

I'm very excited about the prospects of augmented reality across many different fields including education, entertainment, marketing, etc., but the recent *Haagen-Dazs* lid top "Concerto Timer" AR demo – available free in the Apple iTunes store [https://itunes.apple.com/us/app/haagen-dazs-concerto-timer/id670015815?mt=8] is so awful that it's likely to set the entire AR field back a century or two.

The premise is that you take the ice cream container out of the freezer and then you use your phone to download an app and then stand somewhere nearby and watch an AR-generated music video that appears on top of the ice cream container lid for the two minutes that *Haagen-Dazs* thinks you should wait for the ice cream to reach the ideal temperature for consumption.

The only thing that's remotely smart about the whole thing is the hook to a charitable donation for honey bee research and preservation for each of the first 15,000 downloads, but frankly, I'd pay the 5 bucks directly to the charity myself just to have the time back that I wasted on the demo and a promise that I'd never have to try to watch the thing again.

Where should I start?

(1) Who exactly is the audience and how old are they likely to be?

If anyone is experimenting with new, cool AR apps, it's tech-savvy kids and young adults – not grown-ups.

(2) Who thinks that kids today are listening to classical Bach violin pieces?

Bach Inventions No. 14 for violin and cello? Really? Have these guys spent too much time in the freezer?

(3) Who waits 2 minutes for anything today – especially ice cream?

We live in an IG world – Instant Gratification. Waiting for your wine to breath might make sense after you unscrew the lid. My ice cream melts in my mouth.

(4) Who is going to stand anywhere for 2 minutes (like an idiot) holding your phone precisely focused on a pint of ice cream while it "tempers"?

I thought it was painful to watch paint dry. But this is much worse and you only have to watch paint dry once. Here, because the video isn't persistent, it disappears the second you move your phone away from the lid so you have to stand like a mime (while your arm cramps up) to watch something you wouldn't choose to watch on a bet.

(5) Who can even see the image clearly or hear the music being played?

Using *Kinect* to capture the image of the performer rather than playing a clean, simple video (if you absolutely had to) was unnecessary and foolish overkill – like using a sledgehammer to kill a fly – and resulted in bad sound, poor video quality, and overall a completely disappointing experience. What were they thinking?

There are already plenty of intelligent uses of Augmented Reality technologies and some very smart applications that are finally getting traction and which even make good business sense because they supplement and add to the user experience instead of wasting our time. This clearly isn't one of them.

SHOW YOUR USERS THE
SHORTEST PATH

We have always been told (in a quotation wrongly attributed to Ralph Waldo Emerson) that, in terms of innovation, if we built a better mousetrap, the world would beat a path to our door. As it happens, the mousetrap (as we know it today) was invented a few years after Emerson died, but this hasn't prevented the issuance over the last hundred years of thousands of patents for new mousetrap designs along with additional thousands of failed mousetrap applications.

But what's the smartest strategy for a business when the guy or girl next door has already built a better mousetrap? Within reason and the bounds of legality, you'd think that the best plan would be to copy his or her solution and incorporate it into your own processes as soon as possible. Instead, over and over again, whether it's because of our own egos; some unstoppable craving for originality; the "not invented here" syndrome; or just expensive stupidity, we insist on re-inventing even the best wheels.

Now, I'm sure there are instances when pure ignorance is a reasonable defense – if you don't know there's a better way, it's hard to criticize you for not adopting it. I'm also certain that the vast majority of even the most conscientious website managers and marketing gurus don't know that there are new tools being brought to market every day which can help you quickly discover how your business is performing in a competitive context and how your website (or, as I used to call it, "your front door") stacks up against the competitor down the street or across the country. I'll tell you about one of the newest and coolest analytical tools (*Pathful*) in just a moment.

If you're not making it quick and easy for your site visitors and prospects to find quick answers, simple solutions, and a short path to success, you're making your life a lot tougher than it needs to be. And if you can readily determine that your competitors are doing a better job than you are in this area, then the solution is simple. Copy their best approaches and practices and make them your own. Frankly, this is nothing to be ashamed of – it's happened since the beginning of time. This is the reason that there used to be gas stations on 3 or 4 corners of the same intersections or why there are "car dealer" rows and auto parks where competitors sit right next to each other. A good location is a good location. The fact that the other guy may have gotten to that corner first doesn't mean squat unless you're too proud or foolish to park your business there as well.

So what does this mean in the simplest terms for your website? Well, *Pathful* is a new young Chicago-based company that's built some basic tools which can quickly and objectively tell you how effectively your website is doing its job. How well it works – how quickly it gets your customer to and through the point of purchase - because, as they say at *Google*, data beats opinions.

So this isn't a question of how pretty or cool the site is. There's no data point for "cool". And who really cares how much Bob likes it – even if Bob's the boss. His opinion is just that – an expression of one man's preferences and prejudices – not a way to set a smart strategy or build a great business. I'm all for educated guesses and your intuition is sometimes a big help in moving from a "so what?" solution to something spectacular. But start with the facts as your foundation. And that's what *Pathful* can help you do – answer the two most critical questions as to how you're doing and how you stack up against the competition in terms of the operational effectiveness of your site. Getting your customers to their goal so that they give up their gold.

Pathful's analysis addresses and answers a lot of questions and concerns, but the two that always jump out at me (and which are clearly interdependent) are the following: (1) Speed – how quickly can I get to the answers I need? – and (2) Clarity – how clear and free of distractions and detours is the path to success? Here's a simple case in point where 5 different organizations websites (A, B, C, D & E) were tested head-to-head on the Speed spectrum and graphed against Satisfaction. No surprise here – we don't like to wait – we want our answers and we want them now. And the longer we have to wait, the less positive our experience. And, if that wasn't bad enough, keep in mind that this analysis relates ONLY to the people who toughed it out and got to the finish line – not to the large numbers of people who bagged it at various points along the way because it just wasn't worth their time or continued effort or they ran out of patience.

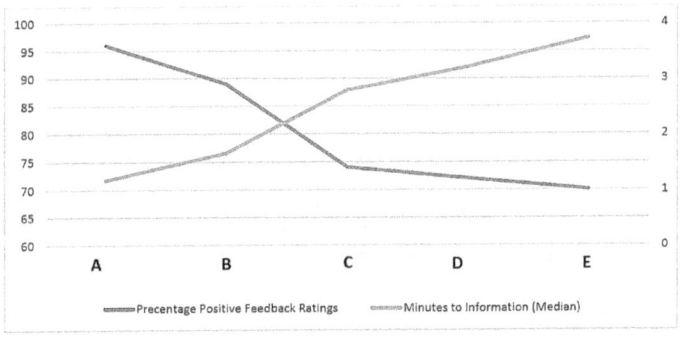

33

COMPARISON OF "SATISFACTION" TO
TIME TO GOAL FOR 5 SITES

The second equally significant component was Clarity and the analysis there was equally instructive. I'm only going to show you the best path and the worst path of the 5 (the displays are a little unwieldy), but you'll get the point. The squares are the right steps and the circles are detours and distractions. These paths proceed from the top of the charts down and – even though each of these two sites had basically 4 steps to get to the finish line – you can clearly see how easy it was for people to lose their way on the worst site – and how often that happened.

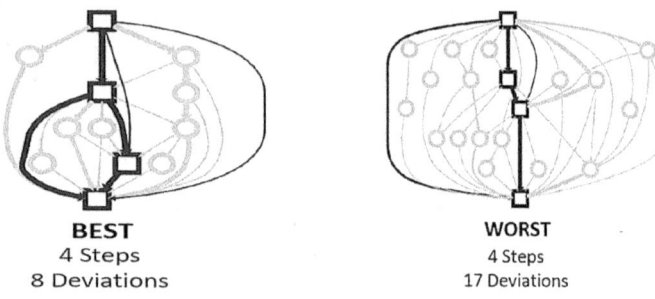

BEST
4 Steps
8 Deviations

WORST
4 Steps
17 Deviations

COMPARISON OF TWO SITES' PATHS TO GOAL

This really isn't rocket science. Think of these charts as potential roadmaps for your business, get in touch with *Pathful* or some other source of comparable and objective data, and get busy.

MAKE MORE MOATS

I'm always surprised how often even very sharp entrepreneurs don't understand the importance of always making sure (through repeated and consistent communication with their team) that, even as their people are chasing new sales opportunities and falling in love with the newest and coolest marketing tools and tricks, they aren't losing their focus on the basic blocking, tackling and execution that help to consistently pay the bills. Essentially this entails nothing more than taking really good care of your existing customers. This may seem a bit old school and even a little boring, but it's a tried and true way to build an increasingly valuable enterprise.

I have always called this basic business strategy "knocking on old doors" which means working harder to deepen your connection to and your involvement with your current customers and thereby to increase their average spend ("share of wallet") as well as to lock them in for the long haul. It's critical for new businesses to always remember that customer churn is the ultimate enemy of increased profitability. In the frenzy of a hot start-up, it may appear that customers are easy to come by because the adoption rate of anything shiny and new these days is remarkably high. But the abandonment rate is 10 times higher than that and if you're not quickly connecting with and retaining these new customers, they'll be gone and you'll be running on a treadmill and going nowhere fast.

Your existing customers (the newest and the oldest) are already in your system and you're already regularly interacting with them (hopefully effectively) so - rather than spending scarce money chasing new customers or trying to steal customers from the competition - you just need to do a better and more expansive job of servicing the guys you've already got and the cumulative results – particularly year over year - will knock your socks off.

It's pretty much a given that happy and "cared-for" customers will simply end up spending more with your company over time. And "organic" customers (basically home-grown) regularly spend LOTS more with better margins than customers acquired through one-off marketing spends, promotions, and other incentives that may attract incremental customers, but don't create lasting connections to them. Think of the pain and suffering caused to thousands of small restaurants by Groupon 1.0 which drew tons of "cheapies", but few returning "foodies".

Happy customers also boost your business and your profits in other ways. They not only buy more (and at better prices); they are also easier and less costly to service; and they're a great and active source of referrals. Especially in the new age of tech-enabled social media, constant connectivity and collaborative commerce, this is the "new" news.

An active, well-run program that drives, encourages and rewards ongoing and authentic customer recommendations and referrals (and incents them to take ownership of the relationship) will generate 5 to 10 times the bottom-line results in terms of actual revenues as any of the other traditional tools including trade shows, print media, and even direct, in-person sales calls. And the results are far more obvious and measurable as well.

You can pretty much forget entirely about trade shows – they're toast. Expensive, inefficient and unfocused: they burn out your people; generate a bunch of worthless leads from lookers, not decision makers; and divert your attention from the things that matter most. If the real decision-makers are even "in the house" at these things these days; you can be sure that they aren't walking the floor and looking for you.

Similarly, in most businesses today, the people still using printed media are so far behind the curve that they might just as well take the money they're spending on creating and delivering print solutions and burn it. In fact, I think – especially in older traditional markets like car sales – that more print/newspaper advertising is driven today by inertia and superstition than by smarts or strategy. You hear older dealers (usually in businesses not run by professional managers) say: "It's how we've always done it – why should we stop now?" Scary, but true.

And frankly, even ignoring the growing presence, utility and efficiency of net-based meetings and demos and video conferencing services, the math today for most products and services simply no longer makes sense or justifies having your sales people on the road trying to sell new customers face-to-face. Wining and dining might be great for your sales people, but from the perspective of busy management personnel in well-run businesses, it went out with the 3 martini lunch quite a long time ago. Good managers want decision-making data about proposed solutions presented as quickly and clearly as possible and they want it now – not in two weeks when the salesman can stop by.

And, if you asked them, your existing customers would also tell you that they're perfectly happy with regular phone updates and new product suggestions or even timely email communications if they are properly managed and valuable rather than just random and unfocused promotional materials. This is known as "the ATM phenomenon". Is there anyone left in the world who would rather deal with a bored and borderline teller rather than a rapid-fire ATM machine for virtually any banking transaction? By and large, if you take a careful look, you'll find that your customers feel pretty much the same about their interactions with you and your sales force. Especially if you have a strong CRM program in place which is primarily focused on capturing the lifetime value of each customer.

But strong, long-term customer connections don't happen by themselves. You need to continually and aggressively work on new ways to keep your customers engaged and invested in the success of your business (as well, of course, as in the success of their own businesses). This process is pretty well understood, although rarely consistently executed.

But the less well-known and clearly under-appreciated tool for customer retention that's even more important because of its competitive deterrence as well as its retention benefits is the need to do everything in your power to increase your customers' switching costs. This is what I call the process of "making moats" which not only keeps your customers in the stable, but also makes it much harder for the competition to reach them and induce them to move. Effective "moats" can come in many forms, sizes and shapes and only you will be able to quickly determine which are the easiest and most cost-effective for you and which make the most sense for your customers.

Keep in mind that I'm not talking here about things like long-term contracts with overlapping expiration dates or similar "legal" constraints which keep folks in the fold. I'm talking about arrangements, value-added tools and data, and other barriers to switching or leaving which arise as a result of things you build and deliver in the ordinary course of your business operations which actually improve the customers' experience and also – as an added benefit – make it much harder for some other competitor or vendor to steal them away.

As I said, the examples are too numerous to list, but there are three industry characteristics which will help you discover and develop the moats which will matter the most in your business.

(1) <u>Complexity</u>

The more that you can do to streamline and simplify essential, but complicated processes for your customers and increase their productivity by saving them time and avoiding redundancy; the "stickier" your connection with them will become. Sometimes these may be complexities built into your own systems, but more likely these are aspects of doing business within a given industry or system where you can accumulate and share – exclusively with your customers – procedures, documents, regulations, and other resources that are necessary to the business, but not necessarily readily-accessible or even known to occasional users. Pre-populated forms; access to associated information like applicable state taxes; drop-down lists and boxes with regularly used choices and selections; embedded estimators and calculators, etc. are all valuable add-ons and the more detailed and industry/user-specific your incorporated add-ons (think of these as "power tools") can be made; the more valuable they will become to your customers and the harder they will be for competitors to replicate.

(2) <u>Compliance</u>

Many industries are more highly regulated than most people can imagine and it takes years of painful and costly experience (often through trial and error) to develop the internal resources and personnel who are sufficiently skilled at navigating these regulatory environments to permit a given company to successfully compete with other established players. But, in many cases, these companies come to rely very heavily on their vendor/partners because a substantial amount of the industry wisdom and compliance knowledge is actually in the hands of the vendors rather than the companies themselves. This is primarily because the vendors are regularly interacting with the state and federal regulators on behalf of multiple clients and parties whereas a typical company's involvement will be much more infrequent and sporadic. The more that you (as a vendor/partner) can add additional functionality and the products of your broader experience to your offerings (turning your "products" into more valuable "services" and consulting), the more locked-in, the customers become.

(3) <u>Consistency</u>

As strange as it may seem from the outside, in many cases, it is often the third-party vendor/partners of large corporations who are the ONLY parties who actually have the data and the ability to advise and assure these large, unintegrated organizations that their various departments, divisions and affiliates are operating in a consistent fashion across the business and in a manner consistent with the company's own rules, regulations and policies. To a certain extent, this is another value-added service where you have the opportunity to provide quasi-managerial functions for your clients who simply don't have the internal capacity or organization (or sometimes the necessary information systems) sufficient to handle these tasks themselves. They really can't tell the left hand what the right hand is doing and they operate at their peril (especially in highly-regulated industries) because of this. As a result and as you begin to gather and archive more and more information about their business's functions and organization, you become an increasingly unique and valuable asset and basically irreplaceable. In an era with increasing management and employee turnover and diminishing institutional memory at all levels, being the keeper of the company's operational history and one of the few places they can turn to assure compliance and consistency throughout their company is a powerful lever for your business and a major deterrent to your competition.

Bottom line: if you want to hang on to your customers for the long run (which is really the name of the game for successful businesses) and go beyond the basic CRM programs that are table stakes these days; you need to erect exit barriers (moats) which raise your customers' switching costs; provide substantial disincentives to migration; and help to exclude competitors. Focusing on their needs to reduce complexity, increase compliance and assure consistency throughout their businesses is the key to keeping them.

Howard Tullman

DON'T WEAR OUT YOUR WELCOME

Having been in sales for most of my adult life (and frankly what entrepreneur isn't always "selling" something), I try to never be rude to even the most clueless or incompetent salesman because I know what a tough and thankless job sales can be. But recently I stopped taking one guy's calls and began just hanging up when he started directly calling my cell phone. (I've also been ducking my barber's calls, but that's a different story.)

All I can say is that I'm very grateful for Caller I.D. these days because – although most of the time I'm strong enough not to hate, this guy was treading on the thinnest of ice. And why? Because he simply wore out his welcome and – with me at least – once you've burned that particular bridge, there's really no way back. Life's just too short to deal with ignoranuses. And, in case that's a new word for you – it's people who are both ignorant and assholes.

But the saddest part of the story is that I went out of my way to give him all kinds of fair warnings. You can't push a rope no matter how hard you try and I fundamentally wasn't interested in what he was selling at the time. Unfortunately, he was just in too much of a hurry to hear me – even assuming (which might be a stretch) that he was interested. The truth is that it's a very thin line between persistence and pestilence, but it's pretty bright and obvious if you're paying attention and listening to what your prospect or customer is saying. This shouldn't be that hard a concept to master.

The fact is that all long-term success in selling always comes from two things – even in this crazy, time-constrained and chronically impatient world in which we are living – building relationships and being patient. And, by the way, I can't believe that I'm saying this – the world's most impatient guy and a long time sufferer of hurry sickness, but it's actually true. Trying to press a sale on an unwilling buyer at the wrong time is a waste of effort and energy. Patience always achieves more in the long run than force and, as I always say, even the strongest "No" is just a "No" for now. But not if you burn down the place and wreck your relationship in the process.

In sales, you're always dealing with people's perceptions which can shift in an instant – they're erratic and discontinuous – so, for a long time, you're it and the next moment, you're out - if you're not careful to thread the needle between obnoxious and irresistible.

I've got a few ideas and suggestions to share with you to help you think about ways to keep the conversation moving forward without crossing the customer's comfort line and throwing out the baby with the bathwater.

(1) Small Serial Successes

Great sales people will tell you that winning is almost never about hitting home runs or bowling someone over in a first meeting with your bravado and BS. It's about solid and consistent base hits – an unbroken series of successful gestures and increments - that lead over time to a relationship based on trust and then a sale. There are times when it's more important to walk away and wait for the real deal than it is to grab a quick sale (whatever your sales manager might think) which may or may not make ultimate sense for the customer. You have to learn to communicate a sense of urgency without seeming to be in a hurry. If you can't move things forward, it's a good time to move on and wait for a better moment.

(2) Someone is Always Selling

As they always say about stocks, they're not bought, they're sold. Selling is about momentum and – at any moment in a conversation – someone is selling – it just might not be you. If you find yourself leaning back on your heels and suddenly on the defensive, you've lost control of the conversation and, most likely, you've just met a master salesman who happens to be your prospective customer at the moment. You always want to be selling from strength and not seeking sympathy or someone's pity. It's OK to agree with your customers and even to empathize with them and all of their problems – as long as you don't end up (with the tables turned) agreeing with their very good reasons for not buying your product or service. And one more thought on this topic – as soon as you start talking about price – you're on the slippery slope and headed in the wrong direction. It's better at that point to pick up your marbles and pack your bags and come back when you're got a better story to sell.

(3) Sell Something Else

When you're selling something that nobody really needs, you'd better actually be selling something else. This is why perfumes are sold by smell, sex and status rather than dollars and cents. And why alarm systems are sold by images of burglars and broken glass – by smoke, security and safety concerns – and almost never on price.

(4) Manufacture "Maybes" and Reasons to Return

In sales, closure is as bad as cancer. A million "maybes" are better than having the door definitely shut in your face. So it's important to always have a plan to prolong the conversation; to have something (however modest) that the customer can say "Yes" to; and to always have a reason to return. Good selling is telling – explaining without a hidden agenda – adding to the customer's knowledge base – and being an impartial source of this type of "education" – and even of juicy industry gossip – is a way to make sure you're welcome to return.

ONE IS THE LOVELIEST NUMBER

Effective competition has always been multi-dimensional. One-trick ponies and businesses that were strong in a single area (product, technology, sales or marketing, etc.) but short in others rarely succeeded in the long run. By and large, there wasn't enough time to fix their shortcomings before the fast followers not only caught up, but quickly provided solutions which were quicker, cheaper, easier to implement or just better designed and more responsive to the real needs of the market.

The first movers and pioneers often identified and defined the problem, developed early approaches and simple solutions, and made all the early mistakes that are always part of the process and they basically set the table. And then, in too many cases to even count, an army of imitators rolled right over them and ate their lunch. One rule will never change – in the end, consumers don't ever care who was first, they only care whose product, service or solution is best when they're buying.

And today, I think it's an even tougher game because some of the fundamental terms of successful competition – especially for start-ups – have changed and the winners (as always) will be the companies that catch on quickly and respond to the new conditions. Sometimes that means moving forward and sometimes that means getting back to basics. These days, we're in a world where there's plenty of capital, there're more than enough customers, and there's even a growing talent pool in many industries and areas.

The competition today is not for capital or resources – it's for the consumer's attention and – for better or worse – you're competing for that attention – not simply with your direct and indirect competitors – you're competing with EVERYTHING that gets in the way of or in front of your message. Don't believe me? Check out your phone (which we do on average 150 times a day) and just scan your messages and news feeds. Family, friends, photos, phonies, ads, alerts, offers – it's unending and filters aren't much help so far. In fact, the initial GOOGLE filters are worse than no help – they actually make more work while you try to find buried messages and important information that some machine or moron at GOOGLE decided weren't worth your time.

It's just a fact of life that the channels to the consumer (and to all of us as well) are congested, confused, clogged, and increasingly costly and it's just way too easy for your message to get lost or drowned in the deluge. Media today is everything that gets in the way of communication. And there's only one thing that could make the situation worse. Spending money that you don't have and can't afford to waste on pushing out a confused or muddled message.

So we're back to that very basic idea that - in communicating with your customers and prospects - getting your message right is even more important than getting your message through. And here's the deal – one is the number. One message, one voice, one spokesman – end of story.

If you're the entrepreneur, I'm hereby giving you permission to tell everyone else to suck on it. It's your show, it's your story, and it's your game to win or lose. And – in the end – it's not about a rampant outbreak of the Egola virus (and don't let anyone else tell you otherwise), it's about effectiveness.

(5) It's Never Everybody's Turn

I realize that a company consists of many people and that many of them are making important contributions to the growth and development of the business. But I just don't care about them or their hurt feelings when they don't get their turn on TV or in the spotlight. Find other ways to recognize and reward their contributions. Democracy isn't a virtue in effective messaging – consistency, image, clarity and communication are all that matter. Let the whiners be the co-captains of the company bowling team.

(6) It's Not Really About You

It's always possible that you aren't the best spokesman for your business or that you're not comfortable in the role. If that's the case, just find the best person you can for the job. I'm assuming that you're smart enough to know your own limitations and desires. (Of course, if you can't successfully sell yourself and your idea, you might just as well forget about being an entrepreneur anyway – although I do realize that the selling doesn't necessarily have to be done on TV or in the spotlight.)

The real point is that – if you do sign up to do this job – it's not an ego thing – it's because it's hard enough to get a clear and concise message out there into the world and the more you can simplify the process - streamline the ideas and the images – and structure the conversations, the more successful you will be. You could teach other people over time to do this, but it's a waste of time in the early stages of the business to even try. Just do it yourself – it's faster and far more impactful.

And keep in mind that delegating your messaging to anyone else – especially outsiders and consultants – is a total disaster. The media may not know much – but they do know the real thing when they see it. And messengers and middle-men just don't work anymore. Like it or not, entrepreneurs today are mini-rock stars and that's who they folks want to see and hear from.

(7) It Really Does Work - Especially for MSM

The media doesn't know anything other than what you tell them. They're lazy and time-constrained. The easier and faster you can make it for them – think one-stop shopping – the happier and more responsive they will be and the more often they will be back. They need "go-to" guys and girls – experts and advocates - not inarticulate amateurs or losers who can't clip on a lav. They don't want a dissertation or a skull session – they want a sound bite. And they're just as grateful to get your message – quickly and easily – as you are to share it with them. Remember that it's not about education – it's about entertainment and selling suds and soup. You're just filler between the ads so they don't all run together. So make your message your ad – short, sweet and smooth.

And that's the drill. Just do it – over and over again – every opportunity you have – obsessively and repetitively. Repeated messages are remembered messages. Stay on message – people take a long time to listen. Don't apologize – don't share the spotlight – don't play nicely with others. Just get out there and get the job done. Even the wanna-be web stars in your company will eventually thank you.

EVERYTHING IS BETTER
BY THE BYTE

F or better or for worse, in today's autocatalytic technology-
driven world, where every change accelerates the speed and
frequency of the changes to follow, gamers (of all ages) are
the virtual canaries in the coal mine. The disruptive innovations
and the market transformations which the gamers' behaviors
consistently predict are felt and rapidly found across every industry
sector and, in general, across the board. As gamers go, eventually
(and increasingly quickly), so goes the rest of the world.

It was the gamers' rapid abandonment of expensive, bulky and
static gaming consoles (Playstation and Xbox) in favor of light,
portable, and mobile devices which not only built companies
like Zynga into almost overnight market leaders, but, much
more significantly, presaged the world's online migration from
the desktop to the mobile world. Mobile today is everything and
everywhere and our smartphones are the direct descendants of
yesterday's handheld gaming devices.

And there's still much more to be learned from the actions and
choices being made by gamers every day which will change the ways
in which more and more businesses price their products and services

and the manner in which they interact with their prospects and customers. We're looking at the end of fixed pricing for anything and entering an ala carte/all the time world. Bulk packaging, bundled products, and even bargain pricing are all breaking down in favor of a single consumer demand driven by a desire for freedom of choice and flexibility – I want "everything by the bite" – whatever I want, whenever I want it, and wherever I am. And it's the gamers who have shown us exactly how these demands will soon find their way into every business.

It's helpful to start by looking at which approaches didn't work over time in the gaming space and why they didn't.

First and foremost, subscriptions and long-term commitments haven't achieved anywhere near the scale and player penetrations that were anticipated. The fundamental reasons are fairly clear – commitments of any kind and continuing obligations are out. Any online game company will tell you that the most active participants won't commit to spend a dollar in advance, but will spend ten dollars – a dime at a time – all day long.

Second, fixed pricing, downloadable paid games and pay-per-play models have also failed. The only companies making real money today (over a million dollars a day in virtual sales) are the companies deploying freemium games where players are charged for upgrades, increased weaponry, powers or skills, or other virtual goods.

So what are the lessons for the rest of us? Three basic propositions underlie the gamers' decision-making process and these ideas are already on their way to your market and your products and services if they're not already there.

First is Investment

The best and smartest games let the users set the effective price of each session or game each time they play. Some days it's a little bit and some days it's a bundle. The point is that the customer is in control. Your pricing strategy needs to incorporate and evidence the same kind of flexibility.

Second is Commitment

The best and smartest games let the users decide how much or little they want to spend each time they play. Some days it's a lot of time or money (each being a material kind of a commitment) and some days it's just a lark to kill some time. If you do things right, you can be all things to all people all of the time. But your products and services need to be accessible across a broad spectrum of pricing and consumer choices and not a simple set of fixed offerings.

Third is Valuation

The best and smartest games let the users decide on exactly how much the experience is worth to them each time they choose to play or continue to play. All the market research and pricing guidance in the world doesn't compare to just letting the customer determine the value of the experience. If your products or services provide real benefit and value to the users, you will discover over time (and over the lifetime of a continued customer relationship) that your best customers will actually pay up for the right experiences rather than try to be bargain basement buyers.

And focusing on the value of the experience is doubly significant because today no one under the age of 30 really cares about possession or frankly about owning anything. Everything is about utility and experience. Social and sharing. Ownership (buying "stuff") is a burden today – not simply because so much of the readily-disposable technology we see and use every day is outmoded and obsolete in roughly the time it takes us to master the things in the first place – but because, in addition, we would just as soon not assume the obligations and the commitments that come as part of the package.

Bottom line – I know that one size, one model, one strategy will never work for everyone – but one thing is true beyond question and that is that your best buyers will tell you that everything is better by the bite.

SMART REACH – BE THERE WHEN THEY'RE BUYING

I've been talking for several years now about how important it is to appreciate that – in today's complicated, ADD-addled, and increasingly cluttered and noisy world – it's become mission-critical in trying to sell anyone anything that marketers understand the new imperative that how, when and where you reach your prospects (and your existing customers) is at least as important as the content of the message you are attempting to deliver.

It's absolutely clear today that the <u>context</u> in which your message is transmitted and received by the target is MORE important to its successful communication and reception than the construction, creativity and even the contents of the message. I call this idea "Smart Reach". Smart Reach is all about the need to deliver engaging, demonstrably relevant, content to your target at exactly the right time(s) and place(s).

And here's an initial hint – in the game today, it's not just about "different strokes for different folks"; it's about fashioning radically and consistently different messages to be directed at the same folks depending entirely on the times and places and contexts in which you're attempting to reach them. And it's also about understanding and appreciating that to do this right; you need an entirely new formula: you should be spending no more than 25-30% of your time and energy of creating new content. The rest of your resources should be focused on planning, channel selection, distribution strategies and real-time measurements of the results so that you can course correct and better shape your campaign as it rolls out.

It doesn't really matter these days whether your content (or offers, incentives, etc.) is the coolest unless it reaches the right audiences. And, because content (standing alone) isn't laser-sighted or heat-seeking; it's gonna need serious help. Just like the fat old chicken sitting on top of the fence post, it's not gonna get there all by itself and it's not gonna get the job done without planning, positioning and an aggressive and focused push from you to help break through the channel clutter and reach the customer.

A staggering number of folks who you'd think were otherwise fairly intelligent don't seem to realize that their literal competitors (the sales folks and businesses who are out there selling directly competitive offerings and competing every day for market share in the same sectors and industries) are only a relatively small part of the problem. You don't get to compete for the sale until you win the race and the constant competition for the consumer's attention.

And in competing for the customer's attention today, which - right along with our time in general - is the scarcest resource we have, the list of distractors, obstructions, barriers and filters just continues to grow larger and longer every day. You're up against family, friends, breaking news, sports, music, medical issues, travel, charities, every kind of media, and even sleep-deprivation. And believe it's hard to sell new shoes to someone taking a snooze or a noon-time nap.

And that's why no one can afford to get these things "almost" right. Today, as always, "almost" only counts in horseshoes and love – not in the marketplace. And almost everything is easier to get into than to get out of – so it's critical to get off on the right foot with the right focus. There's too much money involved, the stakes are far too high, and the consequences if you misfire or waste your ammunition with poorly-timed or poorly-placed salvos are dire. They don't beat you – they just send you home and give the prize to someone else. And I recognize that there's no simple solution or crystal ball to tell you in every case or in any case what the exact right approach should be and that will be a determination that you'll have to make on the fly and over and over again. I certainly don't know and the thing that's for sure is that one size or one approach will never fit every case.

But let me give you just a new idea and a couple of questions to think about as you're analyzing your own programs which I hope will give you a new perspective on the problem. It's a very simple and time-tested idea. You want to be there when the customer wants to buy what you're selling. Because that's the only time that matters and it's a short window that opens and shuts in a snap.

But because you can't really read their minds (yet), you need to settle for the next best thing – smart reach. Think about (a) where you want to engage your targets and (b) what they will be doing when you do and (c) why that's the best possible time for you to make your pitch to them and then figure out how to get your message in front of them – at that time, in that place, and in the context of what they're doing. Reach me at the right time and I'm all yours. Reach me at the wrong time; interfere with or interrupt something that I'm doing which I regard as more important at the moment; get in the way of my friends or family or even my work and you've just wasted my precious time and your scarce and now wasted money.

Context is king.

Howard Tullman

IF YOU WANT TO BEAT BABE RUTH, DON'T PLAY BASEBALL

I wrote recently about "smart reach" and the need to understand that how, when and where you reach your prospects (and your existing customers) is as important as the content of the messages you are hoping to deliver. People who are socializing aren't likely to be in shopping mode; people who are chatting aren't generally consuming; and people digitally scrapbooking aren't really looking for new medications – whether they may need them or not.

These days the context (where they are and what they're doing) often trumps the content (what you're saying or selling) <u>unless</u> your messages get both active engagement from the consumer and are accurately aligned in terms of your target's time, interest and attention. Blindly launching your campaigns into indiscriminate channels (regardless of their aggregate volumes) like *Facebook* where the active users' likely behaviors aren't coincident with the actions you seeking from them is just too sloppy and too costly an approach for virtually any business today. These channels are readily accessible; they may even relatively easy to use and to measure (at least in terms of tonnage but not real reach); and they may not actually appear to cost that much (ignoring the obvious opportunity costs). But there's very little economic benefit in wasting your scarce bullets on bad marketing regardless of the CPMs or per-piece cost. And, frankly, these days the crowd in general is crap. You need to focus on the folks who matter – not the masses – and make your message real for them.

These mega-channels are simply the wrong places to be looking for new business or anything else unless you have thoughtfully crafted and precisely targeted your messages. It's exactly like spending the night looking for your lost keys under the nearest street lamp. Not because that's where you think you lost them, but because the light is so much better there. Lazy marketers use these big fat channels because everyone else is doing the same thing. It's like a drunk uses that same street lamp – for support (and comfort) rather than illumination.

To succeed today, you need real visibility into relevant behaviors and a strategy/plan to move yourself away from the crowd and to do your own thing. If you want to beat the Babe (or the big guys in any business), change the game. That's why, while understanding context is certainly an important consideration to keep in mind and one that you need to take into account when developing your marketing plans, it's only one dimension of the new data and metrics-driven approaches to digital marketing that are changing the game and increasingly distancing the winners from the also-rans.

To really understand what's going on (especially in terms of the ongoing social conversations which, for better or for worse, are impacting your business every day (whether you realize it or not), you need to focus on (a) the multiple dimensions of these social conversations; and (b) who's having them; and (c) who's listening to them in order to spend your time, energy and resources wisely and, more importantly, to be sure that you are targeting and successfully reaching the right audiences.

Today, the fact is that no one with a brain wants to reach millions of easily influenced nobodies – regardless of how many fractured flicks they watch every day or even how many "allegedly" fervent (and generally faithless) followers they may have. Even faithful followers only matter to a marketer if the reason they're following an influencer is directly connected to the messages they're trying to extend and expand. Asking a Justin Bieber fan about Bach is a lot like asking Mrs. Lincoln how she enjoyed the play.

The only goal that really matters today is to get your messages in front of highly influential people (think digital multipliers and megaphones) who are tightly connected to significant (and fairly sizeable) niches of active and desirable individuals whose actions and attitudes they can directly influence (amplification) and whose behaviors as consumers, voters, or other cohort members you are looking to change and direct into actual results – not wishful thinking.

To do this successfully, you need to look at the whole story and at all four of its sides. Even more to the point, the big guys in the social listening spaces (*Radian 6, Buzz Metrics*, etc.) are all myopically focused on just one part of the equation (**WHAT** is being said and the apparent sentiment associated with it) and – as a result – if you hurry, you can jump ahead of them and deliver some valuable and truly-differentiated products and services to a marketplace that is ready, willing and able to buy anything that makes economic sense and that makes common sense out of the tsunami of meaningless data that they're swimming in right now.

As noted above, equally as critical to effective social listening and deliberate message delivery is a determination of **WHERE** the conversations are taking place (context) and information about **WHEN** the conversations are taking place (time). But it's the 4th dimension – the **WHO** is speaking and what are his or her relationships and connections to the ultimate target audiences as well as his or her ability to amplify and extend the messaging thru expressions that sway and influence (power to direct or drive behavior) the targets that is the vast unmined terrain and opportunity zone.

Klout.com and *Kred.com* are the pioneers in the individual influence measuring space, but at best these are mechanical attempts to count frequency, volume and potentially the extent of one's connectivity without a great deal of time or thought being devoted to the true weight, value and influence of the sum of these connections. These are brute force approximations and solutions that are barely workable and of little real value beyond generating some industry bragging rights and hype. This, of course, didn't keep *Lithium Technologies* from buying *Klout* recently for $200 million. I wish them lots of luck in figuring out exactly what they got and what to do with it.

But bigger and better versions of these types of tools are desperately needed because the stakes are high and so – as a result – are the opportunities for new disruptive entrants into this space. It's clear that today even the best language parsing engines and related algorithms are no match for the old family connectivity trees built out of bright colored Post-its tacked to the wall or the white boards that we see every night on the tube in the police procedural shows like *Law and Order*. You can't tell the players without a program and a scorecard and the best computers can still only do our bidding (and massive data assembly), but not our thinking (yet). The companies which build the products and services that help us identify, reach and influence the people who matter (the highly influential and deeply connected prime movers) and who – in turn – can move the markets and the marketplace will be the next generation of big winners.

We don't care about the wisdom of the crowd; we only care about the wisdom of the people we care about.

HOW DO I GET MY APP ON YOUR PHONE?

I sit through lots of meetings these days wondering how so many smart people can be so oblivious to some of the web's harshest realities. They work so hard and they're so creative in most parts of their business and yet they consistently overlook the singly most obvious shortcoming in their plans for global domination. These aren't mediocre mopes or deluded dreamers – they're great technologists, really sharp systems engineers, dynamite designers and even prominent professors. But, far too often, as they pitch their products, services and amazing ideas, what always comes through to me is the sad fact that they just don't get it.

What's the horrendous hiccup? Ya gotta get it out there before it's gonna do you any good. I call it Digital DARE which stands for Distribution, Adoption, Retention and Engagement. If you can't get your mobile application on my phone (distribution) and convince me to initially try it (adoption) and to then keep it on my phone (retention) and finally to use it on a recurring and fairly frequent basis (engagement), you've got nothing to talk about. And each of these steps in the success path presents different challenges and hurdles.

I see this same syndrome with all the new frenzy around content marketing. There's a fierce focus on content creation coupled with "Field of Dreams" fantasies about the ease of digital distribution. The hard truth is that if you're not spending almost as much time thinking about (a) how your message will reach its intended targets (and how you will know [measure] that it has) as you are on (b) developing the message itself, you're just kidding yourself.

In the old days, when we were still talking about desktop computers (before the world moved to mobile), we used to say that "if it ain't on the screen; it don't mean a thing". The point back then was that ideas and talk were cheap whereas execution and delivery were much more difficult. Fascinating features and functions didn't cut it if they weren't in the code base. And all the wonder and wishful thinking in the world wasn't going to get the product shipped and launched. Then, once you shipped your product, the bar was quickly raised again and, at that point, distribution and penetration were the whole ballgame. Yes, that was way back then, but it's just as true and as critical to your success today.

And while the screens we're dealing with may be smaller and much more mobile, the job is still exactly the same. Distribution and adoption are all that matters in the first instance and the competition is tougher than it has ever been because, while there are billions of phones in the aggregate out there in the world, each and every individual user gets to choose what occupies the prime positions on his or her own device. It's just like the real estate business – location and placement are everything. As I've said now for several years - the scarcest piece of real estate in the world is the front screen of the smartphone.

And if you think the adoption curve on cool new technologies is quick; wait until you see how fast these fickle fanatics abandon the latest and greatest anything in favor of the next bright shiny thing coming down the road. Especially anything that's a novelty rather than a necessity. Not only is nothing the future forever; the fact is that it's hard to hang on to a prime position even from week to week without some powerful staying power. The basic rule is: "out of sight, out of mind". Getting there is plenty hard; staying there is harder still. If you're depending on me looking for it; you better be sure that I love it or I'm not gonna make the effort.

So, if you want to be taken seriously (however amazing your application may be), you've got to address the critical concerns which will be front and center in every investor's mind. And while there are no simple solutions, it helps to spend some time thinking about the different ways that you can get over the hurdles and who can help you in the process. Because especially today, these things take tough teams and strategic partners. They never happen by themselves because no one has the time, talent or money to bring it home all alone.

Think along these three dimensions:

(1) Utility - Make It Multi-Purpose

The more functionality that your application provides; the more value it creates for the end user and the more likely it is to succeed. In addition, engagement and retention are frequency games – the more reasons I have to use something; the more instances in which it saves me time or money; the more likely I will be to retain it and keep it close at hand. But don't make it bulky. Feature creep and too many functions is a sure formula for failure. Interestingly enough, excess complexity is exactly why *Facebook* is now slicing and dicing the FB mother lode into a series of single purpose mini-apps. But it's a doomed effort because the sheer number of the individual mini-apps will assure the eventual abandonment of many of them simply because the vast majority of consistent users (MAUs) will pick a couple of core favorites and forget the rest. I realize that it's a straddle, but the winners will be the ones who strike the right balance.

(2) <u>Ubiquity - Make It Multi-Channel</u>

The more channels and locations through which the end users can encounter and obtain your application; the more likely it is to find its way onto their devices. This is all about distribution partnerships and about engineering as many different "win-win" formulations with channel partners as you can manage to put in place. You want to be everywhere the user looks and the "go to" solution for whatever problem or need you're addressing. If you do this right, you're going to spread your application's availability horizontally across the universe of uses in multiple channels and this will provide you another significant advantage against individual vertical channel solution providers who simply won't be able to match the volume and scale that a single multi-channel horizontal solution can achieve.

(3) <u>Universality - Make It Multi-Cultural</u>

You've got to go global from the get-go. Sure the U.S. is a huge market, but it has never been easier or less expensive to make sure that your solution is available and works around the world. I hear stories every day about the power of the web and especially the cloud and how users – acting entirely on their own - are adopting new products or services world-wide without their makers spending any material marketing dollars or trying to put a bunch of feet on the street. Make it easy to go big and broad. Just like the most successful global movies are short on explication and long on explosions; you want your application to be a vehicle that basically doesn't care or even know about the identity, language or other attributes of the content processed through it. This is precisely why photos work so well in so many contexts and sharing applications. What you see is exactly what you get – no more, no less, and no one cares.

YOU DON'T GET A SECOND CHANCE TO MAKE A FIRST IMPRESSION

I call this the *Head & Shoulders* rule: most of the times in business you don't get a second chance to make a first impression and yet that simple fact of life is by no means as obvious and well-understood a phenomenon as it should be. Since we're talking here about "real life" and there are no second acts, rehearsals or do-overs; it's critical to make sure that the first impression people have of you and your business is at least favorable - and ideally - fabulous.

We're designed by nature to make lightning fast decisions (it's all an outgrowth of our earliest "fight or flee" instincts which were developed for self-preservation and to keep the animals we encountered from eating us) and we make these kinds of snap judgments hundreds of times a day without even thinking twice about them or the process. It's a visceral operation – mainly subconscious - and it's far more accurate (in 99% of the cases) than many people and especially behavioral "experts" like to admit. Turns out you can judge a book by its cover. Just not in the ways we used to think about these things.

In the old days, if you wore crappy old clothes to go out and look for a new car (which might or might not have happened to have been clean), the car salesmen would size you up in a flash and basically either ignore you completely or hand you over to the newest and youngest guy on the floor. Today, if you wear those same old duds to go car shopping, after, of course, you've checked everything out first on the Internet, the salesmen can't take the chance that you might be a major "in the money" code monkey or a mobile mega-millionaire and so they have to try to treat everyone who walks into the dealership in the same fashion.

But while this approach might be good rules of the road for the car sales biz and you can get away with dressing like a slob while you're shopping; it's a different story in any social or business context where the decisions you make in terms of your dress, your appearance, or any other aspect of how you elect to present yourself to the world) can influence – for better or worse – other people's impressions of you, your values and your ability to make smart and appropriate choices. People don't know how smart you are when they first meet you; but they can tell in a flash – based in some cases on nothing more than your appearance – that you've made some woefully bad choices sometime in the past. And it's a very short hop from there to "I don't care" or worse.

So we're still judging books and people by their covers – we're just drawing different kinds of conclusions from the data – less about economic circumstances or purchasing power and more about attitude, competence and overall good judgment. This is not to say that you're not always free to ignore other people's impressions and reactions and make your own choices; it's just to remind you that these are, in fact, conscious or unconscious choices that you're making and that all the choices we make come with consequences. And as you get older, you learn that who you are and what kind of life you get to live is largely the sum of all the choices – good or bad – that you've made along the way.

I recently wrote about one part of this problem in connection with the question of what to wear when you go on stage for your Demo Day pitch. See http://www.inc.com/howard-tullman/does-your-demo-rock-how-to-fix-that.html. I thought that your team's t-shirt was probably the safest bet of all, but mainly I was trying to suggest that you stay within the basic guidelines and avoid overdoing it in any direction – you don't want the way you're dressed to become a distraction. And the last thing you want to happen as you walk on to the stage is to have anyone looking <u>at</u> you rather than listening <u>to</u> you.

Crazy clothes, hiked-up heels, and bushy beards all subtract substance, attention and focus from your story. I realize that there are plenty of smart and savvy people who choose to dress or wear their hair in a certain style, but in this narrow context, I think that a fashion *faux pas* can start you off with a crowd that wonders if you're serious. Why would you want to start with that extra monkey on your back? This is a steep enough slope as it is – starting out in a rut of your own making – makes no sense. You should "make your statement" some other time and place.

And there's another monkey that it also makes sense to avoid if you can. Good people (that is to say most consumers) are somewhat patient, largely understanding, and – most importantly – inclined to give almost anyone the benefit of the doubt. But when you present yourself in a fashion that feels more like desperation than design or style; and you put it out there with an "I dare you to say something" attitude; you forfeit the benefit of the doubt.

Now the stakes are changed and you've got to do everything you're doing <u>really</u> well because you've essentially given up the standard margin for error. If you're gonna be right up in my face; you better not slip up because it's a very slippery slope and a very long road back. Make the slightest mistake and the person standing opposite you changes in an instant from "Get Along John" to "Judgmental Joe". People go from neutral to negative in these situations in seconds. We've all been there and done this ourselves.

So if you're gonna have tats all over your body or nose rings in your nostrils; just understand that you're walking a tightrope of your own making. On any given day, you can make it across with no problems, but you've made the job a lot harder and more perilous than it needs to be. And don't think that it's easy to fix the situation or repair the damage with a smile and a few sweet words. You can't talk your way out of problems that you behave yourself into.

WHAT'S REALLY WRONG WITH RETAIL?

W here should I start?

Best Buy is bombing out. They should think about changing the name to Better Buy as in "better buy somewhere else that's gonna be around for the next few years" just in case you need them. It's morphed into a bunch of mini-showrooms for the mobile phone and computer companies and a hands-on demo facility for Amazon shoppers who want to handle the goods before they order online. The increasingly random product mix and the way they change their in-store locations so often make it almost impossible to find anything. It's like a torture maze designed by Conan the Floor Planner. Basically, they're spread a mile wide and an inch deep trying to be all things to all people and to have a little bit of everything for everyone and it's an impossible mission.

The concept of the long tail works – but only in the virtual world - for a simple reason. The web permits <u>infinite inventory</u> which no one in the real world has the cash, the resources or the shelf space to replicate in terms of its breadth or depth of available alternatives and choices. This is one of the main things that killed Blockbuster. Back in the day, we used to call them "Boxbuster" because they stacked tons of empty VHS boxes all over the store to make you think that they actually had something in stock that you wanted to rent (like a hot new hit film) once you asked for it. But when you did ask, nada.

Sears/Kmart (remember Sears?) is also sinking like a stone and they just cut Lands' End adrift for no greater or more apparent reason than they gave when they bought it in the first place. It was a desperate attempt to move upmarket and it went nowhere. Saying doesn't make anything so – you've actually got to change your actions in order to change your culture and to change the public's perception of your position in the market. This stuff doesn't happen overnight even if you're actually committed to making it happen which is somewhat of an open question in Sears's case. Similar attempts to reinvigorate and modernize their sub-brands like Kenmore and Craftsman have also been stillborn. Sears is a proud and historic brand, but it's probably just history these days. Some things are beyond redemption or salvation. Shopping at Sears is a chore and today no one's looking for more work.

And Radio Shack – the original store for geeks, model makers and operators of all sizes and shapes - is a wreck in the midst of the greatest boom in demand for technology and gadgets in history. If anyone had a chance to naturally migrate their business from hobbyists and Trash 80s to the big time in computing devices, it was these guys and they basically got rolled over by everyone else. In addition, with the whole world moving from analog to digital, they completely missed the movement from physical "kits" to digital everything. The Maker movement was their last best shot and they never even stepped up to the plate on that one. At this point, someone just needs to tell these guys to lie down because they are badly burnt toast.

Sears is in no better shape than Radio Shack. Nothing's worked since the Kmart deal. Kmart buying Sears was like taking poison to get even with your enemies and expecting them to die. It's another case of identity loss. Walmart (480B) owns the low price position. You could make an argument that Target (73B) owns the middle-class style and fashion spot although probably not for long – way too many new players moving into that space – and there is no more fickle class of consumers than their targets. And Sears plus Kmart (36B) owns nothing. They have no direction, no passion and no soul. Everything they do these days is short-sighted – it's like wetting your pants in a dark suit. It gives you a warm feeling for a little while, but no one else notices.

How did it happen? First and foremost, they all got caught to varying degrees in the muddle in the middle. Or maybe in the middle of the muddle. Today to compete effectively you just can't be beige or average and their stores and their offerings were basically "so what" in every possible category. If you don't stand for something in the consumer's mind and carve out a demonstrable and defensible niche, you're nothing. You can't save yourself with advertising, promotions, coupons and circulars – these days any kind of "brute force" spray and pray advertising (regardless of the channel) is just the unavoidable cost of being boring. And the proof of the pudding is that there are still companies getting it right. Interestingly enough, they are also still way too reliant on the old-fashioned techniques, but their in-store chops are second to none.

Maybe the best example today is Costco which has clearly figured a bunch of this stuff out. And considering that they started 20 years after Walmart which is the 800 pound retail gorilla, it's impressive that they are doing more sales today (109B) than Target and Sears combined. What exactly do they know that the others don't and why is it important to your business as well?

(1) Family Fun

They've made it fun for the whole family (even Dads) to go shopping again. They've made it an adventure (instead of a chore) to hit the store and see what's new. They get that we're deep into the Entertainment Economy where every environment needs to be immersive, informative and engaging. And they have figured out that the main reason that all the stats suggest that the lion's share of typical consumption decisions are controlled by Moms is because the Dads aren't there most of the time when the shopping takes place. Once you add Dad back into the equation, the average spends of trips where two parents are present (rather than just Mom) increases by more than 40%.

(2) Here Today, Gone Tomorrow

The guys who run Costco are also masters of FOMO – Fear of Missing Out. Every other big box store tells you that they have unlimited quantities of everything to convince you that they will never run out of what you're looking for. Costco convinces you every week that it's your very last chance to grab that item or you'll never see it again. Why else would you buy your Xmas decorations in the middle of October? It's because you sincerely believe that, if you don't, you'll be totally screwed, your family will gleefully remind you of what you missed out on for months thereafter, and you'll be the only one on your block who didn't grab the goods while the gettin' was good.

(3) Run and Gun

They also understand that we all live in a world where IG (Instant Gratification) is the name of the game. I want what I want and I want it now. And they don't leave these things to chance or to even the smartest computers. They know that, while you're waiting in the checkout line, you've got next to nothing to do and that's when their super-salesmen descend with their scanning guns to check out the contents of your cart and let you know how much you will be saving – right then and there – if you switch up to a higher level of membership. In fact, if your order is big enough, you might even come close to covering the annual bump in the membership cost while you're just standing there and – for sure – if you're a regular volume shopper, you'll be miles ahead of the game in just a few weeks. It's easy, it's true, and it's right there – right now.

The moral of the story is pretty clear and simple. The expectations of consumers and customers are progressive – to hold their attention and their affection, you've got to keep making every new visit an adventure and an experience. If you don't, they won't be your customers for long.

Howard Tullman

CARING AND SHARING

A long time ago a very wise old man said: no one cares how much you know until they know how much you care. The ability to consistently demonstrate this type of paramount "personal" and emotional concern to others (about whatever the current issue or matter under discussion may be) is an essential ingredient in the make-up of any successful politician (or husband). We absolutely prefer sweet, "sincere" and somewhat stupid leaders (like Uncle Joe) to serene and severe smarty pants (like President O) who we know in our hearts don't care a fig for us common folk and, basically, would just as soon not dirty their hands dealing with our pedestrian problems. You just can't let those minor day-to-day disappointments get in the way of your grandiose thoughts and big dreams. And if you don't ever deliver on the dreams, well who's really counting anyway – let's just move right along to the next fundraiser.

And, when we (as consumers, customers or an entire country) feel like this, we proceed to act accordingly - by withholding our approval, our support and, most importantly, our commitment. President Obama's functional failings (too many to count) and basic inexperience and incompetence are nothing compared to his complete inability to manage the drama, emotion and theatre of the Presidency in a way that not only instills some (admittedly fast fading) modicum of confidence in his operating abilities, but - much more materially - convinces us that his Spock-ish heart is occasionally in the right place and in our corner. Where's that master of empathy - Doc "Bones" from the Enterprise - anyway when we desperately need him in the dawning age of Ebola?

We don't hear too much these days about anyone being the smartest guy in the room anymore (as if he ever was when either Clinton was within the same zip code), but we do believe that our President's trapped in a womb of his own making surrounded by the same unskilled and useless advisors that he's had around him from Day One plus some guy whose main job is apparently to keep the basketballs inflated at all times. Forget the nuclear football that we used to worry about having close at hand at all times; now it's all about tee times and clean, white Titleists.

You might regard this all as both old news and cheap politics, but managing these types of emotionally-charged interactions and exchanges (where – as often as not – the customers don't tell you the real problem or their actual feelings until: (1) it's too late; (2) the connection with them is irreparably broken; and (3) they're long gone - is also a critical component of how you and your business need to carefully approach the new world of "social" everything where everything's a two-way conversation and everyone gets a vote whether we like it or not.

Today, the context is somewhat different, but the fundamental idea of demonstrating your interest and concern to your intended targets hasn't changed much. The basic objective is to figure out how to make me care and then how to make me share. I'm happy to spread and even amplify your message (as long as it relates to and resonates with me and is delivered at the right time, place and context) by sharing it with my friends and throughout my network as long as I actually believe that the message, the concern, and the process are all authentic. So how do you go about getting it right? And who exactly knows what they're talking about since the majority of the people talking about this stuff have: (a) been doing it for about all of 5 minutes and (b) couldn't find their asses with both hands even if you gave them a hint and a head start.

Sadly, right now, there are about a million people full of suggestions, systems, tools, tips and tricks of the trade for making this whole social thing happen for you – social media consultants are definitely part of a growth industry where there don't appear to be any required credentials although being the biggest blowhard on your block is a definite benefit and being a diva in your own mind doesn't hurt at all either. It also helps to be in your early 20s just as it does in Hollywood where a bunch of equally ill-equipped and uninformed folks are running businesses while they keep looking over their shoulders hoping that no one will figure out that they have no idea what they're doing either.

And then there's also a growing number of morons and scam artists who think that you can "fake it 'til you make it" in this social media business. I'd say they're having roughly the same degree of success as the guys who thought that the makers of Preparation H should also make a lip balm while they were at it. I wrote about these bozos a while ago in these pages. (*The Trouble with Social Media.* http://www.inc.com/howard-tullman/the-trouble-with-social-media.html). Sadly things have only gotten worse with pseudo experts on "virality" being all the rage today. There's a reason that the blind leading the blind don't end up getting anywhere.

I'm not sure that anyone has all the answers for your business (or that the best answers won't change again by next week), but there are three basic ideas that it's important to keep in mind as you develop your own social media plans.

(1) <u>Less Messaging is More Effective
(A Little Goes a Long Way)</u>

Just because you can doesn't mean that you should do certain things. High on that list is inundating your intended targets with tons of repetitive email, interruptive and inconsequential texts, run-of-the-mill offers, mixed and confusing messages, etc. – all of which are doubly destructive. First, by burying your important communications in a pile of non-stop crap, you lose any prospect of commanding the attention of your targets and you also run the risk that your channel may be shut down entirely either by the end-user or by the email guardians in the sky. As the poets used to say, if I had more time, I would have been briefer. Second, by bundling the important material with the mundane and mediocre mass, you cheapen the entire set of messages and make it easier to dismiss your whole effort. There's a reason that people hate bulk mail and it's not just its weight and crappy production values. If you're respectful of my time and interests (and at least semi-polite while you're at it), I'll be happy to help you get the word out.

(2) Give Me Ammo, not Ads (I'll Be Fine)

Information-sharing is a contact sport and it's also a highly competitive one. People – especially those who regard themselves as major influencers in any area – don't just want to know what's going on, they want to be the first to know. But they're not looking for the run-of-the-mill chatter that *Access Hollywood* or *Tech Week* had last week, they want the straight goods and they want the good stuff that will position them as knowledgeable and in the thick of things. Factoids and fluff aren't going to move anyone's needle – you need to develop real facts and substantive information that will stick and stand up to scrutiny and then you need to get it out to your advocates and net promoters as soon as possible - before it all becomes yesterday's news. The bulk of active social sharing now takes place in a matter of hours – the same day - not some days thereafter – and if you miss the first wave, your message will just get lost in the froth that follows.

(3) <u>You Can't Push a Rope (You Won't Have to)</u>

Save your breath and save your money. If you have the right message and a great story, you don't have to sell anyone on selling it for you. The people you want to reach (for their influence and their ability to build your story) – the major influencers in any space - are like the scorpion who rode across the river on the croc's back and then stung him anyway. When the croc asked why (after the scorpion had insisted that he would never do any such thing), the scorpion replied – "it's my nature – it's what I do." Here's the dirty little secret – you don't have to chase or push these folks – just like the scorpion, they also can't help themselves. They have to share and they have to push these stories out there or they fear that they'll no longer be relevant themselves. So don't sweat the distribution part of the program until you've built a rock-solid and valuable story and then let it fly. Sometimes the best push you can provide is to take a step back and watch things happen from the sidelines. Never let 'em see you sweat.

Howard Tullman

LEVERAGING LATERAL LEARNING

I wrote a few months ago about the importance of keeping your eyes open for opportunities to grow and expand your business outside of your core markets and expertise by looking into "adjacent" areas which would afford you the chance to extend your product and service offerings into new geographies and across other dimensions and vectors without substantial new investments or even significant changes in the basic elements of your programs. See http://www.inc.com/howard-tullman/five-reasons-your-market-is-bigger-than-you-think.html.

I called this basic concept "sliding to the side" which meant attacking readily-accessible and proximate markets along new lines which might include identifying and targeting who the new customers were, what the required and desired offerings might be, and/or where, when and how your products and services were going to be delivered in order to meet the needs of the customers and clients in these new markets. This was an idea based on looking outside of your traditional market and sector definitions and then moving in directions that might well be outside of your comfort zone, but which offered rich rewards if you were successful and only modest financial penalties (and probably some wasted time) if things didn't ultimately work out. That was an *inside/out* approach to growing your business.

Equally valuable and again - something that's right before your eyes (if you're looking) – is the idea of lateral learning which is an *outside/in* approach to improving how you are doing things. Basically, instead of working to extend your areas of impact and influence beyond the virtual four walls of your business, here the new idea is that you explore, examine, evaluate and incorporate the best approaches and ideas you can find outside of your own shop and you pull them all into your operations as quickly and seamlessly as possible. You're never going to have all the great ideas yourself or develop all the best solutions internally, so feel free to copy or steal the best of breed answers from anyone and any place you can. Just don't copy their mistakes. Keep in mind that while education is something that is allegedly done to you; learning is something you're responsible for doing for yourself.

I call this concept "lateral learning" and here's the secret: you will absolutely learn as much or more from the people working around you (both in your company and outside) about how to step up your game and improve your prospects as you will from any mentor, teacher, class, book or lecture. When it works well, you discover that you're looking at things you've always thought you've known and understood, but in new and exciting ways. Think of this process as stepped-up and hyper-intelligent osmosis – where you consciously increase the focus and the energy devoted to checking out what and how others are doing things – some even better in the moment than you are – so that you can ultimately get to the point where you look around and no one's kicking your butt or doing your business better than you. Get started today and see what happens. There's no limit to what you can learn if you're not afraid to ask or too embarrassed or shy to inquire. But learning doesn't happen by itself – it's got to be part of an ongoing program and commitment to continually iterating and raising the bar.

And the fact is that you can try this strategy any place and in a variety of ways. But there is no better place to take advantage of learning laterally (from your peers, neighbors, role models and even competitors) than installing yourself in an active and constantly growing startup incubator (like our best-of-breed 1871 facility in Chicago) where there are literally hundreds of businesses in a single massive space and thousands of people working every day to create, develop and grow them every day. When most people talk about why young entrepreneurs should try to get into an incubator (or accelerator), they often focus on some of the obvious emotional components ("it's lonely trying to do this stuff on your own"; "there's a lot of energy and encouragement available in these places; etc.), but it's the serendipitous learning and the amazing synergies and happy accidents that happen every day in these environments that are the things that will really make a difference for you and your company.

And, equally important, the very best incubators aren't glorified coffee shops and co-working real estate plays; they are exceptional places that are purpose-built and run and managed every day to create a constant flood of educational opportunities, critical thoughts, game-changing ideas, new approaches and technologies which change and expand every day because new people are constantly moving in, moving up and/or moving out of the place. They may be growing or about to be going, but the one thing that's for sure is that they are spending every day just like you facing the same kinds of challenges, coming up with new and novel solutions, and suffering all the ups and downs of the startup process that we know and love so well. And you can learn more from them – their bumps and bruises – triumphs, trials and terrors - than from just about any other source.

You might argue that colleges and universities are equally fertile environments for this kind of energy and excitement, information exchanges and aggressive testing of new ideas, and rapid change, but you'd be dead wrong. Sadly, our bulk of our higher education system is about the repeated regurgitation of conventional wisdom and the creation of self-congratulatory dissertations which purport to validate "new" versions of old and tired news. While validation is really important in parking lots, it has very little to do with change, exploration or discovery. And concepts like commercialization, monetization and moving concepts from the labs (and sterile papers and articles) out into the real and very messy world where they can make a difference in people's lives are equally foreign ideas.

In addition, our universities lack just about everything that really matters to the process of disruptive business innovation and new company creation: (a) there's no existential requirement to get some customers and sell something because the professors will always have their jobs and their tenure; (b) there's no sense of urgency to make payroll because they always get a paycheck and there's always another quarter or semester around the corner with a fresh crop of anxious students; and frankly, and most unfortunately, (c) there's absolutely no reward structure in place at any of these places for the slightest risk-taking or for even thinking about making real changes in the way things have always been done. And if the sad combination of those things didn't suck all the juice, mojo and enthusiasm out of these places, it's also downright uncool at college for the "adults" to be passionate and excited about anything outside their academic ivory towers or to be seen as promoting or marketing just about anything. So it's just not happening at So What U.

On the other hand, in an incubator, if you're open to it, you learn by looking, listening and doing every day. This is because you get to free ride on three important trends that are driving rapid and radical change at light speed throughout the tech economy and even in more basic industries as well. Keep an eye out for these 3 drivers:

(1) Solution Migration

What's good for the goose is often just as good and helpful for the gander (except, I suppose, right around Thanksgiving time) and so we are seeing more and more instances where a quick and effective technology solution (or even one that took years and millions to develop and perfect) in one industry (like precision drug dosing cartridges) is ported and rapidly migrates to other industries (like self-service food and beverage providers) overnight and with just as much success and impact. Smart players in almost every major industry (except the U.S. government) have figured this out and are aggressively pursuing these kinds of parallel research and investigation programs. And they're also stepping up to invest in and buy more and more startups as M & A is rapidly becoming the new R & D.

(2) <u>Cross-Industry Pollination</u>

An entirely separate, but equally extensive area for lateral learning is more about behavioral benchmarks and expectations rather than technologies. Seeing what works socially in adjacent businesses; seeing what it's reasonable to ask of and expect from consumers these days and what the *quid pro quo* needs to be; understanding the new dimensions of self-service and constant connectivity; etc. are all inquiries and directions of investigation that are crucial components of how you bring your business to the new digital marketplaces. Just because we haven't previously expected customers to be responsive to certain changes in the way we do business or we have never before asked people to behave in certain new ways doesn't mean that these aren't very significant directions (and potentially opportunities for enormous savings) for your company. The trick here is to let someone else do the first round of experimenting and seeing what and whether anything blows up in their faces before you make your moves. Clearly, as a recent example, the Netflix debacle with Qwikster where they tried for two weeks to split their business into two distinct pieces and almost immediately lost hundreds of thousands of customers and millions of dollars kept a whole lot of other companies from jumping off a similar cliff with their pricing plans. It's always better to let the other guys make the first mover mistakes and then to be a smarter fast follower.

(3) <u>Inexpensive Adaptation</u>

It's not critical or essential that your version of a copied or borrowed solution be gold-plated or crazy expensive at the outset. Try it first with duct tape and chewing gum and see what happens before you bet the farm. You'll learn a lot, maybe you'll lose a little, but you'll never know what can work for you if you don't try. Just don't put both feet into the pond until you know how deep the water is.

Each of these approaches offers value and opportunities for your company as long as you spend the time to think about what they can bring to your business. Keep in mind that the power and value of a change isn't necessarily related to its size. Sometimes the most valuable and important aspect of these things isn't about how much you have to change to make a difference, but exactly how little a change needs to be to make a big impact.

STARTUPS SHOULDN'T SELL STRATEGY

I n the "been there, done that" category of mistakes that you should only make once, I would award a place of high honor to the idea that startups should spend their scarce capital and limited resources trying to "earn" their way into the hearts and wallets of big customers by selling strategy as a door opener. By "strategy," I mean various attempts, presentations, mock-ups, etc. designed to show these big guys the disruptive and scary future and how your company can help them successfully navigate through the coming tough times for their businesses. Here's a flash – these attempts at show and tell (which are really just some smart guys showing off) almost never end well for the little guys – that's you – and, worse yet, it deflects your best people and a lot of your focus in the wrong direction.

I realize that there's an ego component to this stuff and also some bragging rights about who you're pitching and getting in front of. But egos aside, the bottom line is whether anyone is going to be writing you a check any time soon. The method doesn't work, the metrics are always muddled at best, and, for sure, the math is a killer because you rarely get paid anything for the privilege of spending your time chasing these guys. To be successful, you need to develop, design and incorporate your strategies and your solutions into your offerings rather than trying to use them as come-ons and commercials for how well you'll eventually do for the customers.

And, of course, the biggest and saddest joke in this formulation is the word "selling" because - in 99 cases out of 100 - startups aren't selling anything – they're really giving away their time, knowledge and insights for free. Some folks think of this approach as "bread on the water," but I'd say this isn't a loss leader or an intelligent marketing cost; for a startup, I'd say it's much more likely to be a business buster. You end up spending your precious time educating a bunch of folks who often turn out to be indifferent ingrates at the end of the process and politely tell you that (a) they've decided to do it themselves (which we all know that they can't do - even if they steal your ideas); (b) that they're gonna do it elsewhere; or – in many cases because of fear, inertia, or ignorance - that (c) they're not going to do it at all. And only you and your team are that much worse for the wear.

And – if that wasn't bad enough – you'll also learn quickly from your investors (after a couple of these expensive adventures go nowhere) that they thought they were buying into a product or service business and not a consulting firm. They don't want explorers and educators; they want executors. They don't want you strategizing; they want you selling. Fully engaged in turning your ideas into invoices. They're gonna tell you that they'd rather see a month of consistent singles and doubles than wait 3 months hoping for a home run which may never come. As a scrambling startup, you just can't afford that kind of investment.

So forget it. But just in case you can't resist the temptation or the bogus blandishments about how bright you are (think: "that hooker really liked me" in cases of self-delusion like this), here are a few things to keep in mind to help you avoid a total wipeout.

(1) Don't Get Pushed Around

The biggest bullies in big companies are the boys with the least actual power. They can say "No" all day long, but they can't say "Yes" and they know it. They couldn't greenlight a project if their life depended on it - unless it happened to cost a lot less than a latte. So they spend their time taking their frustrations out on you and tormenting young entrepreneurs who don't know any better with big empty promises of good things to come down the line. And – in the meantime – they're only asking for the sun, moon and stars – all for free – because that's pretty much all they've got to spend.

Here's the straight dope: you don't have to give away or prove anything to these guys because they don't matter. Find the folks who can actually sign a check and get in front of them. They're a lot easier to deal with and they can make a real deal happen. They're also a lot nicer too because they don't have a big chip on their shoulders. And they know that - if you want something of real value – you have to pay for it. If you pay peanuts, you get monkeys.

(2) Get Profitable First

Too many complimentary pitches and big bunches of brainstorming freebies will mean too little inbound cash flow and that means trouble for any startup. You need to have an aggressive containment strategy (a limited number of ongoing anythings and that's it) and you need to be sure that your sales team isn't taking the easy way out by selling air and getting paid nothing for it. It's not a "win" when all the commitments and all the costs are on your side of the table. The real focus of management needs to be on making sure that you are identifying and signing up paying customers. The size of the individual deals is nowhere near as critical as the cash. Another important bonus is that these deals don't take as long to launch or as long to complete as many of the bigger ones might.

The truth is that you simply can't afford to pass up the small fish while you're waiting for the whales. See http://www.inc.com/howard-tullman/why-small-wins-beat-big-ones.html. Big companies are one of the last refuges of the slow "No" and there's just about nothing worse for a startup than that. A fast rejection (it only hurts for a bit) is always better than being stroked and strung out by a guy who gets paid to have meetings rather than to make decisions and progress. Once you're making even a little money, you can consider whether to roll the dice on some bigger proposals. Don't be a hurry.

(3) Get A Pilot Project

Don't leave the conversation once you're in the room without something. A trial, a test, a pilot, a prototype, etc. These are all good ways to get the ball rolling, but not for nothing. And equally important you must make sure that there's a clear and express agreement on just what you're committing to do and what exactly will constitute success and the steps to follow afterwards. If the metrics and measurements aren't properly aligned and apparent, you're as likely as not to get to the end of the project and have nothing to show for it because you didn't get the right rules established at the outset.

And don't think that any agreement is better than no agreement because a bad beginning agreement can set the wrong tone for the whole relationship. And don't think that only newbies make these kinds of mistakes. *YouTube* and plenty of celebrities make $300 million worth of these mistakes just a little while ago. See http://www.inc.com/howard-tullman/three-lessons-from-youtubes-programming-disaster.html . So get something, but make sure you know what you're getting yourself into.

(4) Get Paid

If you don't ask, you don't get. You know what your stuff is worth (or you should) and you shouldn't be embarrassed to say that you stopped giving it away for free a while ago. We have all heard the stories about what great reference clients some of these companies will make for your business and these tales are basically BS because everyone in the industry who matters knows that the very same guys make a habit of never paying new companies anything for the chance to test their products or services. They never pick up the check and, after a little while, they start to lose respect for the companies that keep working for free. Just like the patsy in the poker game; if you don't know who it is after 30 minutes of playing (or too many free trials), it's you.

(5) Get Partners Who Are Already in the Door

There are a lot of big companies scared to death these days of everything digital and under tremendous pressure from their own customers and clients to figure things out in a hurry. This kind of demand would be encouraging overall except that these companies simply aren't built for speed in anything and that's where the opportunities are being created for clever young companies with the chops and the technology to get these kinds of jobs done quickly, relatively cheaply and - most importantly - quietly. Think of the big guys as today's Trojan Horses. They're already inside the walls – they have the relationships that would take you years to build with the biggest brands and players around – and they are hurting for help. They can make good partners and you can make them look good as long as you're careful to make sure that your IP and financial interests are protected and that they aren't selling you the same bill of goods about future fortunes that their clients will try to do.

"SMART REACH"
KEEPS GETTING SMARTER

I 've been saying for a while now that the context in which you communicate with your customers is actually more important and material to the success of the communication than the content itself. Your pitch can be Hollywood-quality and utterly heroic, but it will only hit home with those who hear it. We want to be talking to the folks who are willing to listen (and maybe even interested in our story) and not to the accidental observers, the poor suckers who are duped into clicking on random crap, or the people who don't even see our offerings because they're positioned "below the fold" in digital terms. I pity the fools who are still paying millions of dollars for videos "shown", but not seen by any human beings. And I can't wait for the media agencies who are still selling clicks instead of real, measurable results to credulous cretins to take their last desperate breaths and disappear.

In addition, it's increasingly clear that the source of the information and the credibility and connection of the referring/ sharing party matters more than brand, celebrity endorsements, bogus rankings, etc. This is precisely why social is rapidly overtaking search as the primary source of everything we want to know about and why Facebook continues to blow away Google on every possible scale. We want to hear from the people who we know and whose opinions we value and not from the crowd or a bunch of strangers with nothing better to do. In addition, people with broad connections and networks within their organizations or cohorts turn out to have just as much (or more) viral power and amplification capacity as the for-sale "influencers" that everyone has been chasing for the last several years. We just not as dumb any more as the dopes on Madison Avenue continue to think we are. We are looking for authentic, accurate, actionable and timely information to make our buying decisions and it has become a reasonable and realistic expectation that this is exactly what the best and most competitive businesses will provide.

We call this approach "smart reach" – what I want, when I want it, wherever I am, and without asking. And it keeps getting smarter as our data and our tools continue to improve. What has changed the game recently is that the degrees of possible precision in targeting have continued to become more particular, detailed and granular. It's simply no longer sufficient to use proxies, placeholders, and best guesses in order to properly target and reach your audience. In addition, just knowing who the audience is isn't enough information any longer to be the predicate for an effective communication strategy: you've got to know what they are interested in and – even more importantly – when – in terms of their behaviors – when to reach out to them in order to complete the circle.

There's a simple reason that high value products searches are almost all taking place these days on Amazon and not Google or other search engines. When I'm engaged in a defined activity, I go to the power tool for that job – the specialist, not the GP – because I'm time-constrained and I'm trying to get something specific done. I'm not browsing and I'm not bored – it's not a discover exercise, it's a task.

And it's in this mode that the more valuable assistance and offerings you can provide for me (including suggestive selling and "nudge" commerce ideas), the more real value you are providing and the more receptive I am to the pitch. This seems pretty obvious and simple – you're being helpful and additive – not distracting or irrelevant. But it's a message that being missed by the masses of marketers at the moment. If you don't incorporate the mode of my behavior into your marketing model, you're missing the boat.

There's an interesting debate developing right now that addresses exactly these kinds of concerns. It has to do with the fact that – while Facebook has now caught up with (and possibly passed) YouTube in terms of the number of video views per day (call it 4 billion plus a day for each of them) – YouTube argues that the engagement levels of the viewers with each YouTube video are dramatically different and much more substantial and that this "context" makes YouTube a much more attractive channel for video ad placements. YouTube says that Facebook's video "views" suffer from all the same complaints I mentioned above – inadvertent views, distracted viewers, drive-bys, etc. – and that – as a result – the appropriate context for delivering the right video ad to an interested viewer isn't present. But, of course, when the videos you're being shown are sent by your friends and are actually theoretically meaningful to you, you could argue just the opposite - that I'm more likely to watch and be interested and receptive to related video content in this mode – than when I'm bored and scrolling thru random video recommendations on YouTube hoping to find the next great cat video.

In any case, the more major takeaway is that we do many materially different things when we're online (and also we behave differently when we're mobile – which almost everyone is these days – as opposed to when we're sitting in front of a screen) and our attitudes and receptivity to messaging varies as well. In order to reach us effectively, you've got to know how to determine and your plan needs to take into account that my interest in your message will vary greatly depending on whether I'm shopping, gaming, socializing, or just scrolling. Messages that aid and assist me in the process are welcomed – things that interrupt or are irrelevant are ignored.

So the bottom line is pretty simple: if your audience isn't listening, it doesn't matter what you are saying or how well you are saying it. The right pitch at the right point in time and place is the only message that matters and the only one that will make it thru the confusion and the clutter to the customer.

3 THINGS STARBUCKS IS DOING REALLY RIGHT

I had a conversation with a commodities trader recently about Starbucks and how their results have been so impressive over the last year or two. He said that the main reason the stock had done so well was that they were enjoying the financial advantages of depressed commodity prices for coffee. He thought their recent growth was all about their cost structure which frankly – in his opinion - was more a matter of great good luck than anything that they had actively done to manage for this outcome or to achieve these results. I guess when you're a hammer, everything looks like a nail.

I told him that he was totally missing the boat and looking at the wrong metrics and that – because his perspective was off - he wasn't giving the company and their management team anywhere near the credit that they deserved. Interestingly enough, we're drowning in data today, but the sheer increase in available information isn't improving our analytical abilities or helping us (as much as it should) to make better decisions. You can be so focused on particular numbers that it's easy to lose sight of the bigger picture. We think we know what's going on and why, but - on closer examination - it turns out that we're looking in the wrong direction or commending or complaining to our managers about things that are often beyond their control.

Just because some things may look differently these days doesn't mean that anything has actually changed. The bottom line of any good business still grows because its revenues are increased (without an offsetting rise in operating expenses) or because its costs are materially reduced without any sacrifice in the level of its sales. This is the immutable math of margins and it has been ever thus. Nonetheless, it's surprising how often confusion sneaks into this basic equation, alters the correct calculations, and results in inaccurate causal attribution. It may be math, but it's got to be good math and the right metrics to matter.

And even the sharpest managers are guilty of applying versions of the same faulty logic and erroneous explanations - especially when it's in their near-term best interests to do so. In good earnings periods, they're more than happy to take plenty of credit for benefits beyond their bailiwick and in tough times they're pretty quick to blame poor outcomes on bad actors and external forces. I remember when I was selling my computerized resume service to colleges that, in good economic times, the schools bragged on their "job placement" centers, but, in hard times, those same folks took to calling themselves "career guidance" counselors. Actual jobs weren't any longer a part of their jurisdiction.

A lot of this is just human nature, but when you start focusing on or blaming third parties and outside events for your successes or your difficulties, you give up the power to make the kinds of changes which are necessary to continue to improve the situation. Similarly, when you're looking in all the wrong locations for the explanations; you're never going to end up in the right place. The most important job is to illuminate the correct causes so you can eliminate the real problems and so you can also accelerate your commitments to and investments in the things that are actually moving your business forward.

In our conversation, I went on to say, just for starters, that Starbucks had recently raised their prices and that – notwithstanding the sticker shock (as if anyone really noticed or cared except the press) - their customer counts (and, of course, their top line revenues) were still growing. They weren't trying to save their way to success. (See http://www.inc.com/howard-tullman/saving-your-way-to-success-why-you-cant-do-it.html). Frankly, if you're going to take advantage of improved operating efficiencies or available short-term cost savings due to market movements, the smart play is generally to pass those savings on to your customers by reducing your prices to draw more customers in, not to jack your prices up and try to soak the current group. This is the approach which Walmart and Costco have clearly mastered.

And yet, Starbucks seems at the moment to have the best of both worlds. I told my trader buddy that there had to be a better explanation than commodity costs for the kind of pricing power (and price elasticity) that Starbucks continues to demonstrate. My view was that what was improving their overall results was a series of initiatives that the company continued to aggressively advance and that the commodity cost savings were simply additive to, not dispositive of, their overall earnings momentum.

I felt that there were 3 areas where they were just hitting it out of the park and that these were the kind of long-term growth drivers that were driving the continuing appreciation in the Starbucks stock price as well. These are some of the same levers and tools that every startup can also use and which every one of them needs to be addressing as early as possible in their own growth plans.

First, I said that I was impressed with the fact that the number of participants in the Starbucks reward program has grown to over 10 million people and that these "members" spent on average 3 times as much as non-members do. There is nothing better for the bottom line than growing the average ticket of your existing customers. (See   http://www.inc.com/howard-tullman/why-knocking-on-old-doors-is-the-best-sales-strategy.html). They're already inside the tent and now you've just got to show them more attractive opportunities to increase their spend with you while they're there. Virtually no marketing costs and a direct benefit to the bottom line. And loyalty programs continue to pay multiple dividends beyond straight dollars – they drive powerful word of mouth, authentic endorsements, community growth, social media amplification, etc. Every new startup from Day One needs to understand that building a real business is about capturing and retaining the lifetime value of each of those customers which you spend big (and scarce) bucks to acquire and that membership is about much more than just privileges, it's critical to profits as well.

Second, purchases thru the Starbucks mobile app are now accounting for more than 20% of the daily in-store sales. Saves time, saves personnel costs, improves speed and satisfaction – what's not to love? Starbucks (and many other retailers) are rapidly heading in the direction of having their products ready and waiting for you to pick up rather than having you wait for the stuff once you get there. And, of course, it's all about connectivity and mobility. In Europe, the hottest trend ("click and pick") is to order online and then drive to the store to pick up your purchases – often from a drive-thru window. But incorporating a viable mobile solution into your order fulfillment and payment streams isn't as easy as it seems either inside your company (for obvious legacy and enterprise-wide issues) or, more importantly, outside of your company's four walls because it's VERY tough to get the typical consumer these days to add any proprietary app to their already crowded and cluttered phones. You've got to show them a really good reason or try to figure out how to fold your functions into an app that's already there. (See http://www.inc.com/howard-tullman/want-your-app-to-succeed-get-it-out-there.html). This is why Starbucks has such a leg up (with 10 million rewards members) on businesses like McDonald's, for example, who's just trying to get into the game and doesn't really understand the major barriers to adoption which they're facing. The truth is that no one these days really needs another app.

And third, Starbucks keeps adding new complementary products and services offered by on-brand channel partners (NY Times, Spotify, Lyft, etc.) who are dying to get at their affluent and highly-consumptive customers. Having made the acquisition investment, this is a great way to amortize some of their sunk and ongoing costs and still keep growing the overall pie at the same time. It's a lot easier (and much less costly and risky) for third parties to pay Starbucks for this access than it is for them to try to lay their own pipe and reach all of these customers themselves. If the bundles are well done, they can clearly benefit both marketing parties and the consumer. Any business that can become the go-to channel for already assembled concentrations of ready-to-buy customers is in exactly the right place these days to reap the rewards that inure to the gatekeepers and toll takers sitting astride the mobile web. But, here again, you have to be careful that the experience is additive and appreciated by the customers or it's not worth the incremental revenue for your business.

Everything today is about the overall experience and trying to add too much to the process can be a real buzz kill as well as a persistent problem especially when nothing matters more to the customer than getting in and getting out of the place as fast as possible. I want to grab a Venti and vamoose! There's a lot to love about that dolce latte; but my time's much more valuable than your caffe mocha.

Howard Tullman

MAKE ME CARE AND
THEN I'LL SHARE

I have been talking for a while now about an important distinction between the content (message) of an attempted communication and the context (channel and timing) in which that content is delivered. The main objective of smart marketing is to successfully engage the customers/consumers at the right time in a useful dialogue, which has become increasingly two-way and interactive, and not to engulf them in a continual and indiscriminate flood of inappropriate and irrelevant material.

If you get all the elements correct (right time, right place, and right message), you're golden. If you blow it, it means nothing but grief for all concerned. And yet, this basic idea apparently hasn't dawned on millions of marketers who just keep mechanically shoveling their shit our way and who think that there's still some value in sheer velocity and volume. They're dead wrong; they're consistently antagonizing and alienating their audiences; they'll eventually be barred and shut off from these channels, and their clients and companies are paying a heavy price for their ignorance. If they don't quickly change their rationale, their approach and their direction, they'll be left in the dust.

The truth these days is that – given the noise, the clutter and the fierce competition for our fleeting and precious attention – the basic rule of thumb is quite simple: if I'm not listening, it doesn't matter what you're saying. You should save your breath and your bullets for smarter, better and more cost-effective targets. I have previously called this approach the need to focus on "smart reach" and you can catch up on the concept here: http://www.inc.com/ howard-tullman/to-sell-more-your-marketing-must-embrace-smart-reach.html. Basically, you've got to provide each customer with what he or she wants, when he or she wants it, wherever he or she is, and without asking. Otherwise, all bets are off.

But the idea of "smart reach" alone is yesterday's news for those of us who are focused on keeping ahead of the game as well as the competition. The expectations of the consumer are ever changing and progressive (constantly rising). We all know that what may have worked well for us in the past (and, in fact, most of our prior experiences and successes) aren't likely to be relevant to creating tomorrow's triumphs. Just doing the same old things isn't going to make for better results – especially as the competition all around us continues to mount. Experience, in times of radical disruption and change, can be much more of an albatross, a constraint, and a problem for growing businesses rather than something they can comfortably rely upon. See http://www.inc.com/howard-tullman/ navigating-the-information-superhighway.html . And so the moving finger keeps writing new stories and it's those new stories that will create and build the critical connections to the consumer in the future.

And, as smart and aggressive a focus on "smart reach" still may be for many businesses that haven't even begun to advance their thinking; I'm afraid that the bar is jumping up again and that smart reach's time has come and gone as a "be-all, end-all" strategy. This is in part because it's a uni-directional concept (a remnant of the old broadcast "one-to-many" era rather than reflective of our new networked economy) and that's no longer the two-way world we have to operate in. Today all 3 of the main nightly network news broadcasts reach only about 22 million viewers while every day more than 160 million people in the U.S. check in with Facebook. This is the new "many-to-many" environment in which we learn as much or more laterally from our peers as we do from any top-down sources.

Smart reach is all about customized mass communication and individualized messaging, but today we need to think more about our interactions with the customers and consumers as multi-directional conversations: conversations with us, discussions and interactions between interest groups, and third-party sharing among consumers and their peers and influencers as well - in which we will never be direct participants. We know that we couldn't be everywhere the consumer is today even if we tried. And we also acknowledge that we can't service and control every channel to the consumer even with unlimited time and resources. But being there when the buyer is ready to buy is the most critical objective of all. If you can't be found, you will never be chosen.

So the best new strategies have a lot more to do with conversations than simple communications and a lot more to do with advocates and influencers than with advertising and infomercials. This isn't easy for a lot of folks to swallow, no good marketer ever wants to trust his or her fate to others and give up some degree of control over the messaging, but it's easier than you might imagine once you understand that it's no longer about you or your products and services – it's all about them. It's their agenda, they want to drive the process, and you need to figure at least how you can hitch a ride.

If we can't be there ourselves (directly or indirectly), and that's increasingly a given, when these critical conversations and decisions are taking place, then we need to have our messages convincingly and consistently carried forth by authentic and motivated messengers – prompted (but not paid) proxies if you will – who will make it their mission to passionately promote our products and services. Make them care – create a dream that they can adopt and make their own – and let them go forth and spread the word.

Consumers today don't really care to hear anything more about the features and attributes of your products; they want to know how those products will directly benefit them (value) and how they will make a difference in their day-to-day lives (impact). Today we trade our attention for offerings which we believe to have real and specific value for us. Just adding more information to the conversation has no intrinsic value unless it is (a) effectively and credibly communicated, (b) resonates with the target audience, and ultimately (c) impacts and drives the desired behaviors. If you can't make me care about what you have to say, I'll quickly move on to the next best thing. I call this the "show me or see ya" problem.

We really don't have the time or the inclination to do the heavy lifting of learning about new things or ideas these days, but we are willing to briefly listen. And who exactly do we listen to? Some things (like word of mouth) never change and we're still taking the lion's share of the guidance we seek on product and service selections from our friends and peers. But our universe of "friends" has expanded dramatically (and mainly artificially) to include a lot of influencers and others whose opinions and ideas we've come to trust and value even though they would never meet the traditional definition of a friend. Brands used to serve this purpose – as shorthand for quality, value, safety and reliability – but now – given the limited time we all have and the vast amount of choices and the frightening lack of quality decision-making data - we look to loudmouths (not in the pejorative sense), mavens and other mock and manufactured experts to tell us what they think we ought to know. And realistically, to reach these new audiences, these are the folks that you want to deliver your messages for you. And keep in mind that these aren't - by and large – hired guns, flacks, media people or celebrities; they're the ordinary, feet-on-the-street, every day denizens of the web, who are living the new technologies every day, and who the crowd has selected, endorsed and designated as the ones worth listening to.

These folks are a curious breed – passionate about being in the know – passionate about being ahead of the crowd – and most passionate about being in front of a crowd at all times. They live by the doctrine that nothing is real until you've shared it and that everything is better when it's shared. For some it's mostly ego, for some it's a desire to educate, and for the truest believers, it's an almost moral obligation that they feel to share something that has benefitted them with the masses. This is largely their lives (it's definitely <u>not</u> about the money) and they are at it as close to 24/7 as they can possibly be. Here again, in today's short-cycle world, you need people feeding the beast 24/7 on your behalf and these are the ones who seemingly can't help doing just that and couldn't stop doing it if they tried. I call them WOMbots. Word of Mouth "robots". And as peculiar and different as they may seem to us at the moment; they're a lot more likely to have both an immediate and a lasting impact on your business and our future than all the old-line ad agencies and all the new-line social media marketing businesses combined.

Howard Tullman

CRITICAL MASS VS CENTRIFUGAL FORCE

Starting and growing a new business has much more in common with a tornado (and some would say a marriage) than you might expect at first glance. They both begin with a lot of sucking and blowing and, if you're not careful and lucky as well, you could end up losing the house. And while it's never a good idea to bet against Mother Nature or gravity, the good news is that many of the things which are most likely to bring your business down are man-made and sometimes the product of your own actions or – more likely – inactions.

It's increasingly clear that the costs today of true inaction far outweigh the risks of just about anything you're willing to try to do. Keep in mind though that refusing to do things cheaply or quickly or too broadly or before you're fully prepared isn't inaction – it's good decision-making. The things you say "no" to - in the long run - will have a far greater favorable impact on your ultimate success than any quick hits or shortcuts you get sucked into pursuing before you're ready or it's time. Two easy ideas to keep top of mind: don't say "maybe" when you should say "no" and don't try to do something cheaply that you shouldn't do at all.

In addition, these days everyone is an expert on everything and a million people are willing to give you advice – especially when they have no responsibility or liability for the outcomes. (See http://www.inc.com/howard-tullman/expert-advice-is-overrated.html .) Their advice almost always sounds the same: "do something now"; "go big or go home"; "if you snooze, you lose"; "be the first mover", etc. But sometimes the best decision you can make is to say "no" and that's not because you don't want to act – it's because you want to act when and how you choose and when the time is right. It's not always the popular choice or decision, but it's almost always the smart one.

There are certainly going to be some unavoidable risks and existential threats to your company that you'll need to respond to and you're not going to end up anywhere worth going if you try to keep your head in the sand and just creep carefully forward. Things are just moving too rapidly in the global marketplace to act defensively and a go-slow strategy of risk avoidance can be a death sentence for a startup.

But, at the same time, there are also some bumps in the road and some obvious pressures and problems that you can sidestep if you keep your eyes open, pay attention to the signs, and know where to look. The trick is not to let any of these influences (the need for speed, the gospel of scale, the ecstasy of expansion, etc.) and/or influencers (analysts' and media's musings, competitors' and critics' complaints, investors' own agendas, politicians pushing for publicity, etc.) pull your business apart. Screw up your courage, stick to your guns, do what's right for the present, and be ready to flex in the future.

It's really a simple matter of physics. Critical mass actually is critical and it's your job to build or assemble it and to hang on to it. You're pulling everything – all the time – toward the center of things (you're a centripetal "force" – focused, attentive, deeply involved, etc.) trying to hold a lot of things together and the outside (and sometimes the inside) world is constantly conspiring to pull things away from you (they're centrifugal forces – "trying too much too soon", "spreading yourself a mile wide and an inch deep", "trying to be all things to all people", etc.). But as any good entrepreneur knows in his or her heart, you can't have it all. So the trick is to not get tricked into trying.

While many of these concerns are external and market- or competitor-driven, the most insidious ones are from the folks you think are your friends and who technically should be looking out for your best interests. Here's a flash – if they're human and they're breathing, they're looking out for their own interests first. That's just human nature and not a bad thing per se, it's just something to keep in mind as you consider their suggestions and thoughts. A grain or two of salt doesn't just make the soup tastier.

Influencers come in several recurring types, sizes and shapes – watch out for these:

(1) VCs and Aggressive Investors

Most of these guys never met a farm they wouldn't bet and your business (in their minds) is no different. Full speed ahead is the only speed they're interested in and, if you don't make it, they'll be long gone when the layoffs begin. Only moonshots matter and being in the middle of anything is mediocre at best and boring which is even worse. You're trying to build a firm foundation for a sustainable and profitable business and they're trying to find stories they can promote and sell to the next round of greater fools. It's not easy to tell these people to cool their jets from time to time and that your pace doesn't reflect the depth of your passion or your commitment. The best advice I can give you is to try to make sure that you've got some Board members and other advisors (not investors) who've actually run businesses to help take your side in some of the silliest of these arguments. They can help you push back. (See http://www.

inc.com/howard-tullman/why-its-better-when-board-members-back-off.html .)

(2) Politicians

Politicians also love big winners, but they love patronage more and so their primary goals are favorable publicity (no surprise) and spreading the wealth around. As soon as they see a roaring success in the city, they want to put you and your business on the road and have you build copies and clones throughout the state or the country – whether it makes the slightest sense for you to do so or not – because their focus isn't on your progress, prosperity or profits, it's on the populace at large and they see it as the more sites and stories, the merrier. This is a great way to over-extend your business and end up spread so thin that nothing works anywhere and then – of course – it's gonna be shame on you when it all comes tumbling down and they'll be over the next hill chasing the newest shiny story. Rapid expansion is always exciting until it isn't and it's looks easy to everyone who doesn't have to execute the plan.

(3) Media

The media operate on a simple principle – they'll love ya 'til they don't and they're always waiting for you to slip on that banana peel and take a tumble. I realize that they're a necessary evil, but you need to be very careful that you're not saying things or doing things (even worse) to "prove" something to these people because (a) it's never enough to satisfy them in any case and they won't believe you anyway; and (b) it's a fool's errand to waste your time trying to impress people whose livelihood is much more about finding the warts and shortcomings in your story than in celebrating your successes. The best thing I can say about your interactions with most of the media today is the advice I heard long ago about why it makes no sense to wrestle with a pig. Only the pig enjoys it and you just eventually end up covered in mud.

The bottom line is simple: these are all distractions that do next to nothing for your business and are best avoided as much as humanly possible. Keep your head down, keep your eyes on the prize, keep moving forward and all the rest of this stuff will take care of itself if and when it matters at all.

Howard Tullman